MW01092997

Arne & Carlos · Kari Hestnes · Birger Berge
Bente Presterud · Linda Marveng
Iselin Hafseld

KNIT LIKE A
NORWEGIAN

30 Stunning Patterns from Scandinavia's Top Designers

TRAFALGAR SQUARE
North Pomfret, Vermont

First published in the United States of America
in 2021 by
Trafalgar Square Books
North Pomfret, Vermont 05053

Originally published in Norwegian as *Norsk Strikkedesign*.

Copyright @ 2019 Arne & Carlos, Kari Hestnes, Birger Berge, Bente Presterud, Linda Marveng, Iselin
Hafseld, and Cappelen Damm AS
English translation © 2020 Trafalgar Square Books

All rights reserved. No part of this book may be reproduced, by any means, without written permission of
the publisher, except by a reviewer quoting brief excerpts for a review in a magazine, newspaper or web
site.

The instructions and material lists in this book were carefully reviewed by the author and editor;
however, accuracy cannot be guaranteed. The author and publisher cannot be held liable for errors.

ISBN: 978-1-64601-048-6
Library of Congress Control Number: 2020950313

Editor and Coordinator: Iselin Hafseld
Photographer: Eivind Røhne
Stylist: Line Cartridge Lislerud
Interior Layout: Bente C. Bergan
Cover Design: RM Didier
Translation into English: Carol Huebscher Rhoades

Printed in China
10 9 8 7 6 5 4 3 2 1

TABLE OF CONTENTS

PREFACE

Knitting's never been more popular, and the timing couldn't be better. Modern yarns come in a wonderfully wide variety of fiber combinations and colors; traditional knitwear has been rediscovered, revived, and reimagined as cutting-edge contemporary fashion. Inspiration is everywhere. Unlike crafters during the last knitting "wave" in the '80s and '90s, we've got social media, and we're able to share ideas and information like never before. Knitters and designers are able to reach enormous audiences and trade design concepts. There are countless knitting podcasts, blogs, and Facebook groups, plus knitting cafes and knitting festivals. And #knittersofinstagram are too numerous to count!

Interest among young people and those who've never knitted before is growing by leaps and bounds. These days, we're all searching for things that feel real, ways to create something personal, meaningful, and lasting, and knitting is the perfect solution.

Norway has a long-standing national knitting tradition, and the publication of knitting pattern books has exploded in recent years. Nevertheless, it's been over 20 years since the last survey of overall Norwegian knitting design came out. The original Norwegian publisher of this book wanted to change that and got in touch with me. The idea was to gather a bunch of active Norwegian knitting designers who've made their mark in the knitting world and invite them to contribute their unique perspective, creating a unique collection of garments for women and men. The designers we invited were chosen based on their versatility and diverse perspectives; some have been knitting for

decades, and some are just starting to make a name for themselves, and every single one has their own distinct style. But they all share enthusiastic creative energy, and deep respect for both the riches passed down to us by knitting tradition and the possibilities of brand-new pattern innovation.

ARNE & CARLOS are at the top of every list, Scandinavian "knitting rockstars," and contribute their trademark charm and classic style. KARI HESTNES designs colorful, lush garments that catch the eye without fail. BIRGER BERGE reworks traditional pattern elements in stunning new ways. BENTE PRESTERUD presents a selection of designs inspired by bunad (traditional Scandinavian dress). LINDA MARVENG shares her distinctive take on graceful, elegant cables. ISELIN HAFSELD explores both colorwork and cabling with a singular twist.

Each of these contributing designers was allowed free rein to develop their own designs for this book. This freedom is reflected in the wide array of garments and looks, and in the instructions (which include each designer's favored methods for working, assembling, and finishing their pieces). Yarn choice, color, texture, decorative elements, and shaping all contribute to each individual designer's unmistakable signature look. The patterns encompass various levels of difficulty, but most are intended to be as accessible as possible to the inexperienced knitter.

All of us who have come together to create this book hope that it will provide you with endless enjoyment and inspiration, and that it will make you want to knit all the time!

Iselin Hafseld

THE AUTHORS

ARNE & CARLOS are known for their classic and stylish garments, inspired by old knitting traditions and patterns, but also by contemporary street photography. As they themselves say: "We are inspired by our cultural heritage and our handcraft traditions, and try to make them relevant for today's knitters—beloved history with a new twist."

Arne & Carlos's designs are characterized by a combination of elegant simplicity and that special something that's a little more advanced. Everyone can find just the right project for their skill level. The design duo pays close attention to how everything they make can be used. Right now, Arne & Carlos work as freelancers for several large international yarn and pattern distributors. Going forward, they hope to design more patterns for both home décor and clothing collections.

The projects showcased in this book were inspired by old wrought iron door pulls, and acanthus plants in rosemåling (Scandinavian decorative painting done on wood). They also drew on ski sweaters from the 1950s, and last but not least, young

people in contemporary photos wearing sweaters they found in drawers and closets at their grandparents' homes.

KARI HESTNES is a designer who welcomes challenges with open arms. Many of the garments she designs are rich in color and combine multiple motifs, but with a grace and attention to detail that create harmony. As she herself says: "Colors have always fascinated me, and I love to play with new shades and combinations in my designs."

Kari's designs are distinguished by her delight in art and fashion, and her desire to make wearable everyday garments; her patterns demonstrate her versatility and sense of style. She's inspired by the possibilities of quality yarns and rich colors, but also by other types of art. She works as a freelancer and takes commissions from many different customers. In addition, she spends a great deal of time on her other passion, painting.

Her designs in this book were inspired by the way light falls on summer evenings, and by Frida Kahlo's gloriously saturated

colors and paintings inspired by folk art.

BIRGER BERGE is a young designer well-known for the way his garments combine the modern and the traditional. Many of his patterns showcase his interest in the rich textile traditions we have in Norway. As he says, "Traditional motifs are often intimidatingly intricate; I try to find the underlying simplicity and purity, and use that in my designs."

Birger's patterns are characterized by their modern look, often with traditional colors livened by a splash of something unexpected. He often chooses a theme and creates several different expressions of and variations on it, and is inspired by shifting light as well as colors drawn from nature and old textiles. He designs in his free time.

His work for this book was inspired by the rich knitting and textile traditions found in Norway's Vestland and Selbu regions.

BENTE PRESTERUD is a designer always open to new ideas, full of inspiration. Her garments give her a way to explore her fascination for pattern combinations and exciting contrasts. And, as she says, "I like to make things in new ways—I think it's fun and inspiring when a pattern makes you pay closer attention or discover some unexpected details."

Bente's collections have a sense of holistic coherence that stands out. Some of her designs do tend to be a little challenging—but not impossible—for the novice knitter. She likes to experiment with shaping, colors, and details, and is often inspired by folk costume traditions. Bente works freelance and takes commissions from many different customers, which means she gets to let her creativity take her lots of different directions.

Her designs for this book were inspired by folk costumes and traditional patterns, as well as by Hardanger embroidery, Selbu roses, and elegant bunad (Norwegian dress inspired by traditional rural clothing).

LINDA MARVENG is known for her elegant and feminine silhouettes and fashion-saturated looks. Many of her garments are born of her interest in art and architecture. As she says: "I often find inspiration in fashion photography and cityscapes, as well as colors in nature, art, and textiles."

Linda's designs are characterized by sculptural and flattering lines that show how fascinating textures can be created with intricate pleats and panels. For Linda, good fit is important, so her garments are often seamed; finishing this way can be time-consuming, but the results are strikingly beautiful. Linda works freelance and takes commissions from many different yarn producers. She sells her designs to both international and Norwegian magazines.

Her designs in this book were inspired by Celtic mythology, high-quality yarns, and old wood carvings.

ISELIN HAFSELD is famous for timeless and lovely garments that display her ingenuity and desire to create. Her designs showcase her ability to work intuitively and with variety. As she says, "Inspiration for new designs can come from all kinds of sources, colors, and structures—one thing or another that sets the creative process in motion."

Iselin's patterns are characterized by her sense of fashion, design, and movement. Her priority is creating wearable, good-quality clothing, and this governs her choice of materials and approach to garment shaping. She's always on the lookout for new and exciting modes of expression that take designs further. Iselin works under her own clothing label, TINDE, and takes individual commissions freelance.

Her designs in this book were inspired by woven textiles, and Aran patterns from weather-beaten and windy landscapes.

JENNY'S PULLOVER

SKILL LEVEL
Experienced

SIZES
S (M, L, XL, XXL)

FINISHED MEASUREMENTS
Chest: 36¾ (39½, 42¼, 44½, 47¼) in / 93 (100, 107, 113, 120) cm
Total Length: 24½ (25¼, 26, 26½, 26¾) in / 62 (64, 66, 67, 68) cm
Sleeve Length: 17 (17¾, 18¼, 18½, 19) in / 43 (45, 46, 47, 48) cm

YARN
CYCA #2 (sport, baby) Hillesvåg Ask (100% Norwegian wool, 344 yd/315 m / 100 g)

YARN COLORS AND AMOUNTS
MC: Light Warm Gray 316106: 350 (400, 450, 500, 550) g
CC1: Farmer Red (Bonderød) 316013: 50 (100, 100, 100, 100) g
CC2: Blue-Gray 316104: 50 (50, 50, 50, 50) g

SUGGESTED NEEDLE SIZES
U. S. sizes 2.5 and 4 / 3 and 3.5: long and short circulars; set of 5 dpn

GAUGE
24 sts x 32 rnds in stockinette on larger needles = 4 x 4 in / 10 x 10 cm.
Adjust needle sizes to obtain correct gauge if necessary.

KNITTING TIPS
Some places in the colorwork pattern have long stretches between color changes. To avoid long floats, twist the colors on the wrong side every 3-5 stitches—but make sure not to stack these twists with one directly below the next, or the unused color will show on the right side.

BODY
With MC and smaller circular, CO 224 (240, 256, 272, 288) sts. Join, being careful not to twist cast-on row; pm for beginning of rnd. Work around in k2, p2 ribbing for 2 in / 5 cm (all sizes). Change to larger circular and continue in stockinette until body measures approx. 12¼ (12¼, 12¾, 12¾, 12¾) in / 31 (31, 32, 32, 32) cm. Now work in pattern following Chart **A**. Begin as shown for your size (front) and work the repeat from A to B around. Work in pattern to the underarm marker for your size. Pm at each side with 111 (119, 127, 135, 143) sts for front and 113 (121, 129, 137, 145) sts for back. BO 5 sts on front at each side marker and 6 sts on back on each side marker = 11 sts bound off centered at each side for underarms. Set body aside while you knit sleeves.

SLEEVES
With MC and smaller dpn, CO 48 (48, 52, 52, 56) sts. Divide sts onto dpn and join; pm for beginning of rnd. Work around in k2, p2 ribbing for 2 in / 5 cm (all sizes). On the last rnd, increase 4 (6, 8, 10, 10) sts evenly spaced around = 52 (54, 60, 62, 66) sts. Change to larger dpn and continue in stockinette.

Sleeve Shaping
Size S: Increase 2 sts centered on underarm every 5th rnd 14 times = 80 sts. Continue in stockinette until sleeve is 12¼ in / 31 cm long. There are no increases in the section with pattern knitting.
Size M: Increase 2 sts centered on underarm every 5th rnd 17 times = 88 sts. Continue in stockinette until sleeve is 13 in / 33 cm long. There are no increases in the section with pattern knitting.
Size L: Increase 2 sts centered on underarm every 5th rnd 18 times = 96 sts. Continue in stockinette until sleeve is approx. 13¾ in / 35 cm long. There are no increases in the section with pattern knitting.
Size XL: Increase 2 sts centered on underarm every 4th rnd 10 times and then every 5th rnd 11 times = 104 sts. Continue in stockinette until sleeve is 14½ in / 37 cm long. There are no increases in the section with pattern knitting.

CHART A

Size XXL: Increase 2 sts centered on underarm every 4th rnd 11 times and then every 5th rnd 12 times = 112 sts. Continue in stockinette until sleeve is 15½ in / 39 cm long. There are no increases in the section with pattern knitting.

All sizes: When sleeve is 12¼ (13, 13¾, 14½, 15½) in / 31 (33, 35, 37, 39) cm long, begin pattern following Chart **A**. Begin as shown for your size and work the repeat from A to B around. Work in pattern to the underarm marker for your size. Pm in first st of rnd on right sleeve and last st on left sleeve. BO marked st and 5 sts on each side of marker = 11 sts bound off centered on underarm = 69 (77, 85, 93, 101) sts rem. It is important that you bind off on the same round in pattern as on the body. Set first sleeve aside while you knit second sleeve.

YOKE

Arrange pieces on larger circular, placing markers as follows: (marker 1), first sleeve (marker 2), front (marker 3), second sleeve (marker 4), back = 340 (372, 404, 436, 468) sts total. Continue in pattern, shaping yoke at the same time.

Raglan Shaping: Knit 1 rnd without decreasing. On the next rnd, decrease as follows: at marker 1: k2tog, knit until 2 sts before marker 2, sl 1 as if to knit tbl, k1tbl, psso, k2tog, knit until 2 sts before marker 3, k2tog, sl 1 as if to knit tbl, k1tbl, psso, knit until 2 sts before marker 4, k2tog, sl 1 as if to knit tbl, k1tbl, psso, knit until 2 sts before marker 1, sl 1 as if to knit tbl, k1tbl, psso = end of rnd. Decrease the same way on *every* rnd 3 (4, 5, 6, 6) times = 316 (340, 364, 388, 420) sts. Now decrease on *every other* rnd 19 (22, 23, 25, 27) times = 164 (164, 180, 188, 204) sts rem. Either bind off or place on a holder, the center front 25 (27, 27, 27, 29) sts for front neck. Now work back and forth. Continue raglan shaping as est and, *at the same time*, BO or place on holder 1 st on each side at neck edge on every row 5 (6, 7, 7, 7) times = 35 (39, 41, 41, 43) sts on front neck. After completing Chart **A**, continue with MC only. Place all sts for front neck on larger circular and knit 1 rnd, adjusting stitch count to 92 (100, 100, 104, 108) sts. Change to smaller circular and work around in k2, p2 ribbing for approx. 1 in / 2.5 cm. BO in ribbing.

FINISHING

Seam underarms. Weave in all ends neatly on WS. Pat out sweater to finished measurements and place between two damp towels or lightly dampen and lay out on a towel until completely dry.

AKSEL'S PULLOVER

SKILL LEVEL
Experienced

SIZES
S (M, L, XL/XXL)

FINISHED MEASUREMENTS
Chest: 42½ (46½, 51¼, 55½) in / 108 (118, 130, 141) cm
Total Length: 27½ (28¼, 28¾, 29¼) in / 70 (72, 73, 74) cm
Sleeve Length: 18¼ (18½, 19, 19¼) in / 46 (47, 48, 49) cm

YARN
CYCA #2 (sport, baby) Hillesvåg Ask (100% Norwegian wool, 344 yd/315 m / 100 g)

YARN COLORS AND AMOUNTS
MC: Black 316053: 400 (450, 500, 550) g
CC1: Natural White 316057: 100 (150, 150, 150) g
CC2: Red 316071: 50 (50, 100, 100) g

SUGGESTED NEEDLE SIZES
U. S. sizes 1.5 and 2.5 / 2.5 and 3: long and short circulars; set of 5 dpn

GAUGE
24 sts x 32 rnds in stockinette on larger needles = 4 x 4 in / 10 x 10 cm.
Adjust needle sizes to obtain correct gauge if necessary.

KNITTING TIPS
Some places in the colorwork pattern have long stretches between color changes. To avoid long floats, twist the colors on the wrong side every 3-5 stitches—but make sure not to stack these twists with one directly below the next, or the unused color will show on the right side.

BODY
With MC and smaller circular, CO 244 (272, 296, 320) sts. Join, being careful not to twist cast-on row; pm for beginning of rnd. Work around in k2, p2 ribbing for 2 in / 5 cm (all sizes) and then 2 rnds in ribbing with CC2 and 2 rnds in ribbing with MC. The ribbing will be about 2½ in / 6 cm long for all sizes. On the last rnd, increase evenly spaced around as follows:
Size S: Increase 1 st in every 15th st 12 times, every 16th st 4 times = 260 sts.
Size M: Increase 1 st in every 19th st 8 times, every 20th st 6 times = 286 sts.
Size L: Increase 1 st in every 18th st 8 times, every 19th st 8 times = 312 sts.
Size XL/XXL: Increase 1 st in every 18th st 14 times, every 17th st 4 times = 338 sts.

Change to larger circular and continue in stockinette with MC until body measures 15 (15¾, 16¼, 16½) in / 38 (40, 41, 42) cm. Pm at each side with 129 (143, 155, 169) sts for front and 131 (143, 157, 169) sts for back. Continue in pattern following Chart 1. Begin as shown for your size, repeating from A to B around. When body is approx. 4 in / 10 cm shorter than total length, BO (or place sts on a holder) the center 17 (19, 19, 21) sts on front for neck. Now work back and forth and, *at the same time*, on every other row at neck edge, BO 2, 2, 1, 1, 1, 1, 1, 1) sts = 37 (39, 39, 41) sts for neck. When body is approx. ¾ in / 2 cm less than total length, BO (or place on holder) the center 29 (29, 31, 31) sts of back neck. Work each side separately. On every other row at neck edge, BO another 3, 2 sts = 39 (39, 41, 41) sts rem for back neck. After completing Chart 1, change to smaller needles and, with CC2, work 2 rows in stockinette. BO rem sts. Work the other side the same way.

SLEEVES
With MC and smaller dpn, CO 52 (52, 56, 56) sts. Divide sts onto dpn and join; pm for beginning of

CHART 1

B   repeat   A   M   L   XL/XXL   S

☐ MC
■ CC2
☐ CC1

CHART 2

B   repeat   A

* center of sleeve
▨ MC
▤ CC2
☐ CC1

rnd. Work around in k2, p2 ribbing for 2 in / 5 cm (all sizes). Now work 2 rnds with CC2 and 2 rnds with MC; the ribbing should be approx. 2½ in / 6 cm long for all sizes. On the last rnd, increase 5 (7, 7, 7) sts evenly spaced around = 57 (59, 63, 63) sts. Change to larger dpn and continue in stockinette with MC.

Sleeve Shaping: Increase 2 sts centered on underarm on every 8th rnd 9 (8, 8, 9) times and then on every 6th rnd until there are 93 (95, 97, 99) sts. When sleeve is 14¼ (14½, 15, 15½) in / 36 (37, 38, 39) cm long, work in pattern following Chart 2. Count out from center of sleeve to determine where pattern will begin, making sure pattern is centered on sleeve. When sleeve is total length, turn sleeve inside out and work back and forth in stockinette for facing. Work 2 rows with CC2 and then continue with MC until facing is approx. ¾ in / 2 cm long. BO loosely. Set first sleeve aside while you knit second sleeve.

FINISHING
Turn sweater inside out and lightly steam press on WS. Measure top of a sleeve across width. Use that measurement to mark depth of armhole at each side. Machine-stitch a double line of medium-length stitches on each side of center armhole stitch. Carefully cut open each armhole. Seam shoulders.

Neckband: With MC and smaller circular, pick up and knit a multiple of 4 sts around neck. It will be neatest if you begin at one shoulder. With MC, knit 1 rnd and then work 1 rnd k2, p2 ribbing with MC. Next, work 2 rnds ribbing with CC2, and then continue ribbing with MC only until neckband is 1½ in / 4 cm high. BO in ribbing.

Attach sleeves and sew facings down on WS to cover cut edges of armholes. Weave in all ends neatly on WS. Pat out sweater to finished measurements and place between two damp towels or lightly dampen and lay out on a towel until completely dry.

KRISTIN AND KRISTIAN'S ACANTHUS COWL

SKILL LEVEL
Experienced

SIZES
One size

YARN
CYCA #2 (sport, baby) Hillesvåg Ask (100% Norwegian wool, 344 yd/315 m / 100 g)

YARN COLORS AND AMOUNTS
MC: Dark Brown Heather 316103: 100 g
CC: Natural White 316057: 50 g

SUGGESTED NEEDLE SIZES
U. S. sizes 2.5 and 4 / 3 and 3.5: 24 in / 60 cm circulars

GAUGE
22 sts in pattern on larger needles = 4 in / 10 cm. Adjust needle sizes to obtain correct gauge if necessary.

KNITTING TIPS
Some places in the colorwork pattern have long stretches between color changes. To avoid long floats, twist the colors on the wrong side every 3-5 stitches—but make sure not to stack these twists with one directly below the next, or the unused color will show on the right side.

With MC and smaller circular, CO 144 sts. Join, being careful not to twist cast-on row; pm for beginning of rnd. Work around in k2, p2 ribbing for 2 in / 5 cm. Change to larger circular and work following chart. After completing charted rows, change to MC only and smaller circular. Work around in k2, p2 ribbing for 2 in / 5 cm. BO in ribbing.

Weave in all ends neatly on WS. Gently steam press cowl (but not ribbing) under a damp pressing cloth.

CC Natural White
MC Dark Brown
Heather

MAGNE—MEN'S ACANTHUS MITTENS

We drew two charts for these mittens, one for the right hand and the other for the left hand. We know that many knitters find it tricky to mirror-image a chart so that thumb ends up in the correct place for each hand.

SKILL LEVEL
Experienced

SIZES
One size

YARN
CYCA #2 (sport, baby) Hillesvåg Ask (100% Norwegian wool, 344 yd/315 m / 100 g)

YARN COLORS AND AMOUNTS
MC: Dark Brown Heather 316103: 50 g
CC: Natural White 316057: 50 g

SUGGESTED NEEDLE SIZES
U. S. sizes 2.5 and 4 / 3 and 3.5: sets of 5 dpn

GAUGE
24 sts in pattern on larger needles = 4 in / 10 cm. Adjust needle sizes to obtain correct gauge if necessary.

KNITTING TIPS
Some places in the colorwork pattern have long stretches between color changes. To avoid long floats, twist the colors on the wrong side every 3-5 stitches—but make sure not to stack these twists with one directly below the next, or the unused color will show on the right side.

With MC and smaller dpn, CO 50 sts. Divide sts onto dpn and join; pm for beginning of rnd. Work around in k2, p2 ribbing for 2½ in / 6 cm. Change to larger dpn and work following chart up to line marked with X. On the rnd for the thumbhole, on the dpn with thumb sts, place all sts not used for thumb on a new needle and knit 13 thumb sts (between the red lines) with smooth, contrast color scrap yarn. Continue around from the X in pattern. Now read chart as usual, from right to left. Finish the mitten by cutting the yarn and drawing end though rem 10 sts; tighten.

THUMB
Insert a dpn through the 13 sts below scrap yarn and another dpn through the 13 sts above scrap yarn. Carefully remove scrap yarn. Pick up and knit 1 st at side of thumbhole, k13 in pattern, pick up and knit 1 st at side of thumbhole, k13. Continue, following chart, shaping top as shown on chart. Finish the thumb by cutting the yarn and drawing White end though rem 8 sts; tighten.

Make the second mitten the same way, following respective chart.

Weave in all ends neatly on WS. Gently steam press mittens (but not ribbing) under a damp pressing cloth.

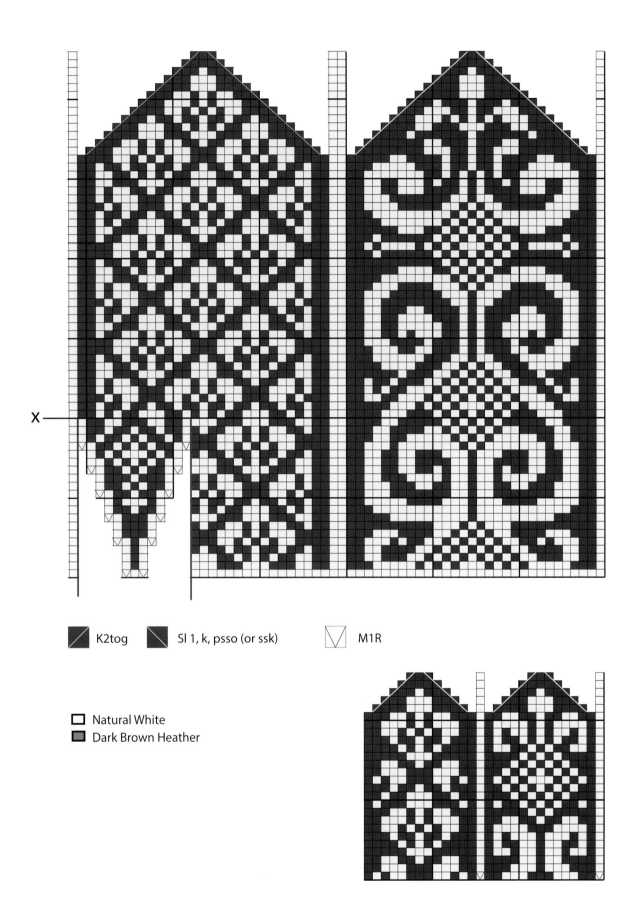

X —

| ◼ K2tog | ◪ Sl 1, k, psso (or ssk) | ▽ M1R |

☐ Natural White
◼ Dark Brown Heather

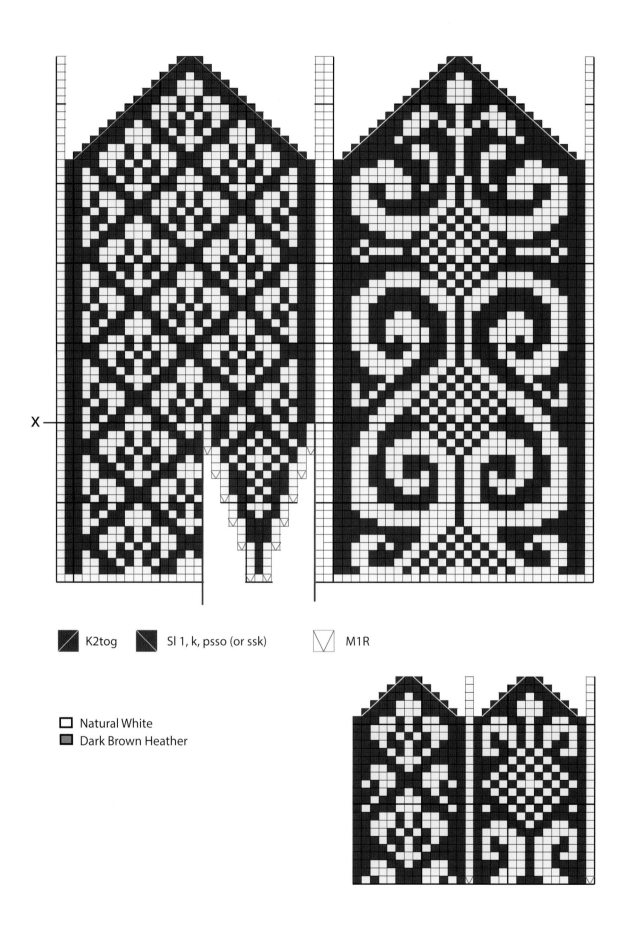

X

| K2tog | Sl 1, k, psso (or ssk) | M1R |

Natural White
Dark Brown Heather

STINE'S PULLOVER

SKILL LEVEL
Experienced

SIZES
S (M, L, XL, XXL)

FINISHED MEASUREMENTS
Chest: 36¾ (39, 41¾, 44½, 47) in / 93 (99, 106, 113, 119) cm
Total Length: 24½ (25¼, 26, 26½, 26¾) in / 62 (64, 66, 67, 68) cm
Sleeve Length: 17 (17¾, 18¼, 18½, 19) in / 43 (45, 46, 47, 48) cm

YARN
CYCA #2 (sport, baby) Hillesvåg Ask (100% Norwegian wool, 344 yd/315 m / 100 g)

YARN COLORS AND AMOUNTS
CC1: Cognac Brown 316140: 100 (100, 100, 100, 100) g
CC2: Beige 316142: 150 (150, 200, 200, 200) g
CC3: Dark Coral Red 316111: 150 (200, 200, 200, 200) g
CC4: Light Yellow 316119: 100 (100, 100, 100, 150) g

SUGGESTED NEEDLE SIZES
U. S. sizes 2.5 and 4 / 3 and 3.5: long and short circulars; sets of 5 dpn

GAUGE
24 sts x 32 rnds in stockinette on larger needles = 4 x 4 in / 10 x 10 cm.
Adjust needle sizes to obtain correct gauge if necessary.

BODY

With CC1 and smaller circular, CO 222 (238, 254, 270, 286) sts. Join, being careful not to twist cast-on row; pm for beginning of rnd. Work around in k1, p1 ribbing for 2 in / 5 cm (all sizes). Change to larger circular and knit 2 rnds. Pm at each side with 111 (119, 127, 135, 143) sts each for front and back. Work around in pattern following Chart 1. Begin at side of front, repeating from A to B to marker at opposite side. Begin again as shown and rep from A to B to end of rnd.

Note: The pattern will not match at the sides (the center front and back are marked on the chart; make sure pattern is centered on front and back).

After completing Chart 1, continue in stockinette with CC2 until body measures 9½ (9¾, 9¾, 10¼, 10¾) in / 24 (25, 25, 26, 27) cm. Now work following Chart 2. Begin at side of front, repeating from A to B to marker at opposite side. Begin again as shown and rep from A to B to end of rnd. After completing Chart 2, continue in stockinette with CC3 until body measures 17 (17¾, 18¼, 18¼, 18½) in / 43 (45, 46, 46, 47) cm. BO 5 sts on each side of each side marker = 10 sts centered at each underarm. Set body aside while you knit sleeves.

SLEEVES

With CC1 and smaller dpn, CO 48 (48, 52, 52, 56) sts. Divide sts onto dpn and join.
Work around in k1, p1 ribbing for 2 in / 5 cm (all sizes). On the last rnd, increase 3 sts evenly spaced around = 51 (51, 55, 55, 59) sts. Change to larger dpn and knit 2 rnds. Work around in pattern following Chart 1. Count out from the center to determine where the pattern begins for your size. Make sure pattern is centered on sleeve.

Sleeve Shaping: On every 8th (7th, 6th, 6th, 5th) rnd, increase 2 sts centered on underarm = 81 (87, 93, 99, 105) sts.

After completing Chart 1, continue in stockinette with CC2 until body measures 9½ (9¾, 9¾, 10¼, 10¾) in / 24 (25, 25, 26, 27) cm. Now work following Chart 2. After completing Chart 2, continue in

CHART 3

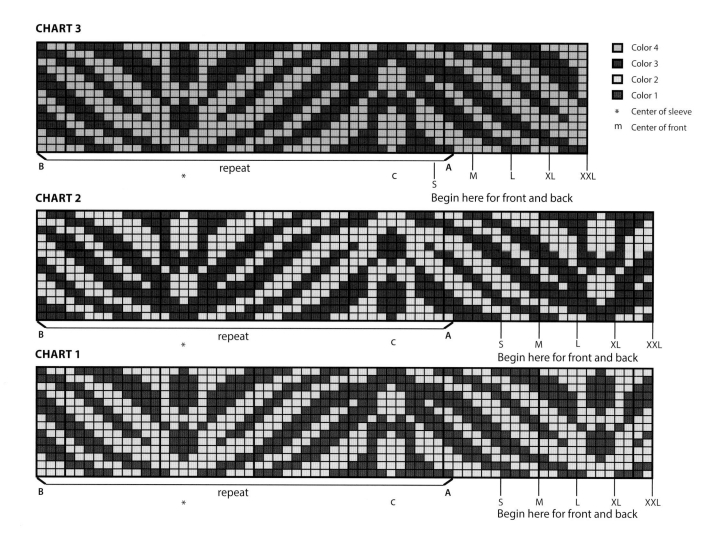

Color 4
Color 3
Color 2
Color 1
* Center of sleeve
m Center of front

B   repeat   C   A   M   L   XL   XXL
*   S
Begin here for front and back

CHART 2

B   repeat   C   A   S   M   L   XL   XXL
*
Begin here for front and back

CHART 1

B   repeat   C   A   S   M   L   XL   XXL
*
Begin here for front and back

stockinette with CC3 until body measures 17 (17¾, 18¼, 18¼, 18½) in / 43 (45, 46, 46, 47) cm. BO 10 sts centered on underarm.

Set sleeve aside while you knit second sleeve the same way.

YOKE
Continue with CC3. Arrange pieces on larger circular as follows: Pm 1, first sleeve, pm 2, front, pm 3, second sleeve, pm 4, back = 344 (372, 400, 428, 456) sts total.

Raglan Shaping: Knit 1 rnd without decreasing. On next rnd, decrease as follows: At 1st marker: Sl 1 as if to k1tbl, k1tbl, psso; knit until 2 sts before 2nd mark-

er, k2tog, sl m; sl 1 as if to k1tbl, k1tbl, psso; knit until 2 sts before 3rd marker, k2tog, sl m, sl 1 as if to k1tbl, k1tbl, psso; knit until 2 sts before 4th marker, k2tog, sl m, sl 1 as if to k1tbl, k1tbl, psso; knit until 2 sts before marker 1, k2tog = end of rnd. Rep this rnd once more = 328 (356, 384, 412, 440) sts. Now work following Chart 3. Mark center of each sleeve and count out to determine beginning of rnd. Begin on front and back as shown, and, *at the same time*, continue decreasing for raglan as est. The pattern will not match at raglan lines. Rep the raglan decreases on *every* rnd 1 (2, 3, 4, 4) times more = 320 (340, 360, 380, 408) sts rem. Now decrease on *every other* rnd 19 (22, 23, 24, 26) times = 164 (164, 176, 188, 200) sts rem. After completing Chart 4, continue in stockinette with CC4.

BO or place on a holder the center front 27 (27, 27, 29, 31) sts for front neck. Now work back and forth. Continue raglan shaping and, *at the same time*, BO or place on holder 1 st on each side of neck on every row 5 (6, 7, 7, 7) times = 37 (39, 41, 43, 45) sts for front neck.

Neckband: Slip all neck sts to smaller circular. With CC4, knit 1 rnd, adjusting st count to 92 (100, 100, 104, 108) sts. Change to CC1 and knit 1 rnd and then work around in k1, p1 ribbing for about 1 in / 2.5 cm. BO in ribbing, making sure bind off is not too tight.

FINISHING

Seam underarms. Weave in all ends neatly on WS. Pat out sweater to finished measurements and lay between 2 damp towels until completely dry or dampen sweater and lay out to finished measurements on a towel until completely dry.

WINTER BRIDE

When I was given the honor of contributing to this book, I wanted to make something I had never made before, and chose a bridal outfit. I wanted it to be feminine and pretty and, at the same time, to include a connection to Norwegian knitting traditions. The crown is from my art project, *Wheels of Life—a Pilgrimage to Inner Wisdom*; there is no pattern for it.

SKILL LEVEL
Experienced

SIZES
S (M, L)

FINISHED MEASUREMENTS
TOP
Chest: approx. 34¼ (36¾, 39) in / 87 (93, 99) cm
Waist: approx. 28 (29½, 32¼) in / 71 (75, 82) cm
Length: approx. 19¾ (20½, 21¼) in / 50 (52, 54) cm
SKIRT
Total Length: approx. 39½ (40¼, 41) in / 100 (102, 104) cm; the skirt stretches a bit in length when blocked
Total Length of Knitted Skirt: approx. 42½ (43¼, 44) in / 108 (110, 112) cm
Circumference: at lower edge, approx. 76 (84¼, 108¼) in / 193 (214, 275) cm
The waist/lower edge can be adjusted with ribbon through the eyelets.

YARN
CYCA #0 (lace) Mondial Kid Seta (70% super kid mohair, 30% silk, 230 yd/210 m / 25 g)
CYCA #2 (sport, baby) Mondial Giada (70% Merino wool, 30% silk, 153 yd/140 m / 50 g)

YARN COLORS AND AMOUNTS
Color 1: Giada Light Rose 831: 200 (200, 250, 250) g
Color 2: Giada White 100: 150 (150, 200, 200) g
Color 3: Kid Seta White 100: 225 (250, 275, 300) g
Color 4: Kid Seta Powder Pink 391: 200 (225, 250, 275) g

SUGGESTED NEEDLE SIZES
U. S. sizes 1.5, 2.5, 4, 6, and 8 / 2.5, 3, 3.5, 4, and 5: circulars

CROCHET HOOK
U. S. sizes B-1/C-2 and G-6 / 2.5 and 4

NOTIONS
10 small buttons to match dress color
2.75 yd / 2.5 m, ⅝ in / 1.5 cm wide silk ribbon to match dress

GAUGE
30 sts in pattern with Giada on U. S. 2.5 / 3 mm needles = 4 in / 10 cm.
23 sts in stockinette with Kid Seta held double on U. S. 2.5 / 3 mm needles = 4 in / 10 cm.
17 sts in lace pattern with Kid Seta on U. S. 6 / 4 mm needles = 4 in / 10 cm.
14 sts in lace pattern with Kid Seta on U. S. 8 / 5 mm needles = 4 in / 10 cm.
Adjust needle sizes to obtain correct gauge if necessary.

TOP

Note: The top can be worn with the buttons down the front or back. The photos show a version buttoned down the back; the pattern describes how to make one with buttons down the front.

Begin working back and forth. With U. S. 1.5 / 2.5 mm circular and Color 1, CO 246 (266, 286) sts.

Lace Panel: Knit 2 rows = 1 garter ridge.

Make an eyelet row: K1, *k2tog, yo 2 times, k2tog tbl, k1*; rep * to * to last st and end k1.

Knit 4 rows. On the last row, adjust st count to 245 (269, 287) sts by decreasing 1 (increasing 3, increasing 1) st evenly spaced across. At the end of the row, CO 6 sts = center front steek—purl these sts throughout.

Now join to begin working in the round. Pm as follows: 6 steek sts = center front, pm, count 50 (54, 58) sts, pm = right front, count 21 (23, 25) sts = side sts, pm on center side st and pm after side sts. Count 103 (115, 121) sts = back, pm, count 21 (23, 25) sts = side sts, pm on center side st and pm after side sts. Count 50 (54, 58) sts, pm = left front.

Pattern: The pattern on Chart **I** is worked on U. S. 2.5 / 3 mm needles, with a stripe pattern on the side panels. Work in pattern on the right front: see arrow on chart for where to begin your size. *K1 in Color 1, k1 in Color 2* over side sts; rep * to *, ending with k1 in Color 1. Work pattern on back: see arrow on chart for where to begin your size. *K1 in Color 1, k1 in Color 2* over side sts; rep * to *, ending with k1 in Color 2. Work left front mirror-image to right front. Always purl the 6 center front steek sts with Color 1. Work 2 more rnds the same way.

Shaping Sides: Work until 1 st before center st of right side panel, sl 1, k2tog, psso. Decrease the same way on the left side panel. Decrease the same way on every other rnd a total of 9 (10, 11) times on each side = 209 (229, 243) + 6 steek sts rem. Continue without decreasing until body measures 4 (4¼, 4¾) in / 10 (11, 12) cm. Now increase 1 st at each side of markers on side panels on every 4th rnd 12 (12, 13) times = 257 (277, 295) + 6 steek sts. Continue without increasing until body measures 11½ (11¾, 12¼) in / 29 (30, 31) cm.

Shape Armholes: Work around until 6 sts before side marker, BO 11 sts, work until 6 sts before next side marker, BO 11 sts and work to end of rnd. Now work each side separately.

Right Front: Continue in pattern, working back and forth. *At the same time*, at left side, on every other row, BO 2 sts 2 times and 1 st 2 times. Then, on every 4th row, decrease 1 st 4 times.

Front Neck Shaping: When 4 in / 10 cm before total length, shape neck on right side of front. BO 17 (19, 21) + 6 steek sts. Next, on every other row, at neck edge, BO 3 sts 2 times, 2 sts 2 times, and 1 st 10 times. When ¾ in / 2 cm from total length, shape shoulder by binding off from the outer edge of shoulder on every other row 4-4-4 (4-5-5, 5-5-6) sts. No sts rem at shoulder.

Left Front: Work as for right front, reversing shaping to correspond.

Back: Continue in pattern, working back and forth. Shape armholes as for front, binding off at each side of back.

Back Neck Shaping: When 4 in / 10 cm before total length, shape back neck by binding off the center 39 (41, 43) sts. Work each side separately. Next, on every other row, at neck edge, BO 3 sts 2 times, 2 sts 2 times, and 1 st 10 times. Work straight up until same length as front for shoulders and shape shoulders as for each front.

FINISHING
Weave in all ends neatly on WS. Lightly steam press on WS under a damp pressing cloth. Seam shoulders.

Reinforce steek by machine-stitching 2 lines, 1 zigzag, 1 straight stitch, on each side of center steek st. Carefully cut steek open up center st. Fold edges in along a stitch column and baste down to hold in place while you do the rest of the finishing.

Crocheted Edgings for Armholes: With smaller hook and Color 1, beginning at side of body, work 3 rnds sc around armhole. Change to Color 2 and work 1 rnd sc.
Picot Edge: Work *1 sc, ch 1, 1 sl st in same st, 2 sc*; rep from * to * around. Cut yarn and fasten off securely. Crochet the edging around the other armhole the same way.

CHART I

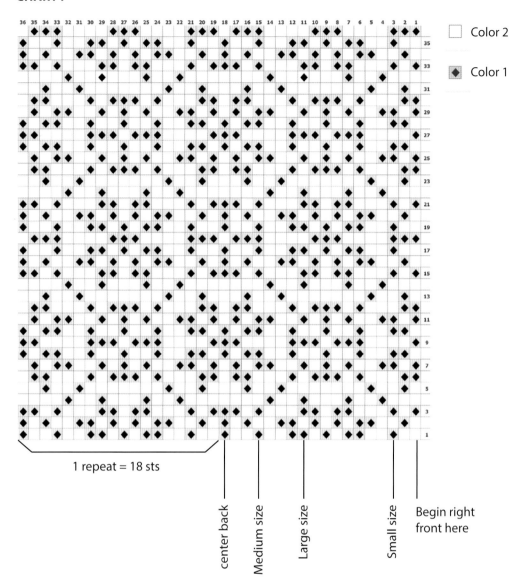

1 repeat = 18 sts

center back
Medium size
Large size
Small size
Begin right front here

Color 2
Color 1

CHART II

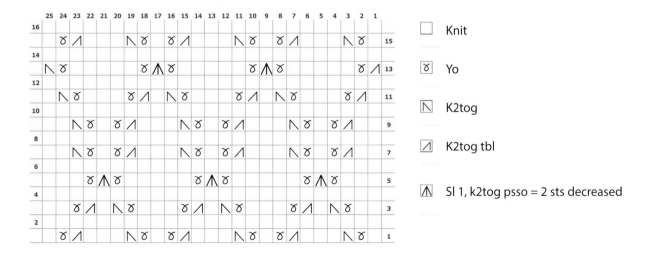

Knit

Yo

K2tog

K2tog tbl

Sl 1, k2tog psso = 2 sts decreased

31

Crocheted Edging for Neck: With smaller hook and Color 1, beginning at neck on right front, work 3 rnds sc. Change to Color 2 and work 1 rnd sc.
Picot Edge: Work *1 sc, ch 1, 1 sl st in same st, 2 sc*; rep from * to * around. Cut yarn and fasten off securely.

Crocheted Left Front Band: With smaller hook and Color 1, beginning at left front neck, work 3 rows sc along front edge. Change to Color 2 and work 1 row sc. Cut yarn and fasten off securely. Mark placement for 10 buttons.

Crocheted Right Front Band with Buttonholes: With smaller hook and Color 1, beginning at right front neck, work 2 rows sc along front edge. Make buttonholes on next row: Place top buttonhole 2 sc below upper edge, bottom one 6 sc above lower edge, with the rest spaced evenly between. For each buttonhole: Ch 4, skip 3 sc and work 1 sc in next sc. On next row, work 3 sc in each ch loop.

Turn and work 1 row sc with Color 3. Work picot edge as for armholes. Cut yarn and fasten off securely.

Crocheted Edging for Top: With smaller hook and Color 2, work 1 row sc and then picot edge as described above. Cut yarn and fasten off securely.

SKIRT

The skirt is worked in several layers that are knitted together as you proceed.

1st Ruffle: With circular U. S. 8 / 5 mm and Color 3, CO 337 (369, 385) sts. Join, being careful not to twist cast-on row; pm for beginning of rnd. Knit 1 rnd, purl 1 rnd, knit 1 rnd, purl 1 rnd. Continue around in stockinette until ruffle is 15¾ in / 40 cm long. Work next rnd as follows: *k2, k2tog*; rep * to * around, ending with k1 = 253 (277, 289) sts rem. Change to circular U.S. size 6 / 4 mm and work around in stockinette for 2½ in / 6 cm. Set piece aside.

2nd Ruffle: With circular U. S. 8 / 5 mm and Color 4, CO 337 (369, 385) sts. Join, being careful not to twist cast-on row; pm for beginning of rnd. Knit 1 rnd, purl 1 rnd, knit 1 rnd, purl 1 rnd. Continue around in pattern following Chart **II**. Make sure you begin with the first 8 sts on the chart, working the repeat until 9 sts rem, and then work last 9 sts on chart. Continue around as est until ruffle is 15¾ in / 40 cm long, ending with either Row 5 or 13 of chart. Work next rnd as follows: *k2, k2tog*; rep * to * around, ending with k1 = 253 (277, 289) sts rem. Change to circular U.S. size 6 / 4 mm and Color 4 and knit 1 rnd.

Joining Ruffles: Hold 1st ruffle behind 2nd ruffle and knit them together as follows: knit 1 st from 1st ruffle together with 1 st of 2nd ruffle. Continue joining the same way until all the sts have been joined. Knit around in stockinette for 2½ in / 6 cm and the set piece aside.

3rd Ruffle: With circular U. S. 6 / 4 mm and Color 3, CO 337 (369, 385) sts. Join, being careful not to twist cast-on row; pm for beginning of rnd. Knit 1 rnd, purl 1 rnd, knit 1 rnd, purl 1 rnd. Continue around in pattern following Chart **II**. Make sure you begin with the first 8 sts on the chart, working the repeat until 9 sts rem, and then work last 9 sts on chart. Continue around as est until ruffle is 15¾ in / 40 cm long, ending with either Row 5 or 13 of chart. Work next rnd as follows: *k2, k2tog*; rep * to * around,

ending with k1 = 253 (277, 289) sts rem. Change to circular U.S. size 2.5 / 3 mm and knit 1 rnd.

Joining Ruffles: Hold 3rd ruffle over the ruffles you've already joined, and knit them together as follows: knit 1 st from 3rd ruffle together with 1 st of 2nd ruffle. Continue joining the same way until all the sts have been joined. Holding one strand each of Colors 3 and 4 together, change to U. S. 2.5 / 3 mm circular, purl 1 rnd and then continue in stockinette. Knit without shaping until skirt measures a total of 39½ (40¼, 41) in / 100 (102, 104) cm. Knit 1 rnd, *at the same time* decreasing 7 (11, 3) sts evenly spaced around = 246 (266, 286) sts. Change to circular U. S. 1.5 / 2.5 mm and Color 1. Knit 2 rnds.

Eyelet Rnd: Work k1, *k2tog, yo twice, k2tog tbl, k1*; rep * to * around, ending with k1. Knit 3 rnds and then BO.

Crocheted Edgings:
With larger hook and Color 1, work 3 rnds sc around lower edge of 1st ruffle.
With larger hook and Color 2, work 3 rnds sc around lower edge of 2nd ruffle.
With larger hook and Color 3, work 3 rnds sc around lower edge of 3rd ruffle.

You can arrange the outfit in several ways. First decide whether you want it to button on the front or on the back. Once you've decided that, you can choose whether to place the bow on the front or on the back.

Put the skirt on under the top so that the eyelet panel on the skirt lines up behind the eyelet panel on the top. Now thread the ribbon through the eyelet holes. Begin where you want the bow to be tied. Tie a neat knot and cut ribbon to desired length. We suggest wearing a tulle skirt under the dress to give it a little volume. If you want sleeves on the top, you can find a pretty blouse to wear with it. You can wear this dress for parties, or pair the top with another skirt in your wardrobe.

✦ FRIDA'S LONG FALL JACKET

A few years ago, I had a thought: I wanted to make a series of knit designs inspired by the life and art of the Mexican painter Frida Kahlo. That was the beginning of a whole new inspiration for me to play with patterns and colors. After that, many Frida designs followed—including this long jacket, with a lovely rose panel at the lower edge framed by ribbed edges and sleeves. The jacket has subtly shaped sides and will look lovely on most body types.

SKILL LEVEL
Experienced

SIZES
S (M, L, XL, XXL)

FINISHED MEASUREMENTS
Chest: approx. 36 (38½, 41, 44½, 48¾) in / 91 (98, 104, 113, 124) cm
Lower Edge Circumference: approx. 44½ (47¾, 50¾, 55½, 60¼) in / 113 (121, 129, 141, 153) cm
Total Length: approx. 37 (37¾, 38½, 39½, 40¼) in / 94 (96, 98, 100, 102) cm
Sleeve Length: approx. 19¼ (19¾, 19¾, 20, 20) in / 49 (50, 50, 51, 51) cm

YARN
CYCA #2 (sport, baby) Hillesvåg Ask (100% Norwegian wool, 344 yd/315 m / 100 g)

YARN COLORS AND AMOUNTS
Color 1: Dark Brown Heather 316103: 350 (350, 400, 400, 450) g
Color 2: Dark Fly Blue 316136: 200 (200, 250, 250, 250) g
Color 3: Pink 316135: 100 (100, 150, 150, 150) g
Color 4: Dark Terracotta Heather 316503: 50 (100, 100, 100, 100) g
Color 5: Ochre 316133: 50 (50, 50, 50, 50) g
Color 6: Olive Green 316090: 50 (50, 50, 50, 50) g

SUGGESTED NEEDLE SIZES
U. S. sizes 1.5 and 2.5 / 2.5 and 3: circulars and sets of dpn.

You may want to use U. S. 4 / 3.5 mm needles for the stranded colorwork.

CROCHET HOOK
U. S. size B-1/C-2 / 2.5 mm

NOTIONS
7 wood buttons to match jacket
Approx. 2.4 yd / 2.2 m ribbon to cover cut edges of steek behind front bands.

GAUGE
24 sts in pattern on U. S. 2.5/4 / 3/3.5 mm needles = 4 in / 10 cm.
24 sts in stockinette on U. S. 2.5 / 3 mm needles = 4 in / 10 cm.
Adjust needle sizes to obtain correct gauge if necessary.

Note: Read through the entire pattern before you begin knitting, as several steps may be worked at the same time. Also, be sure to read the information on the charts. If you knit stranded colorwork tightly, go up a needle size and knit a swatch first to make sure your gauge is correct.

BODY
The body is knitted in the round.

Lower Ribbed Edge: With circular U. S. 2.5 / 3 mm and Color 1, CO 272 (292, 312, 342, 367) sts + 6 sts for center front steek (the steek sts are not included in stitch counts; always purl steek sts). Work around in p2, k3 ribbing, ending with p2) for 3½ in / 9 cm. Knit 1 rnd, and, *at the same time*, decrease 1 (1, 3, 3,

0) sts evenly spaced around = 271 (291, 309, 339, 367) sts. Pm at each side with 66 (71, 76, 83, 90) sts for each front + the 6 steek sts between the two fronts and 139 (149, 157, 173, 187) sts for back.

Pattern Following Chart I: Work in pattern following Chart **I** (change to a needle one size larger, if necessary to obtain gauge). Begin at arrow for your size and rep pattern around. Work 1 repeat in length.

Pattern Following Chart II: Work in pattern following Chart **II**. Begin at arrow for your size and rep pattern around. Work 1 repeat in length.

Pattern Following Chart I: Work in pattern following Chart **I** (change to one size larger needle if necessary to obtain gauge). Begin at arrow for your size and rep pattern around. Work 1 repeat in length.

Pattern Following Chart III: Work in pattern following Chart **III** (change to one size larger needle if necessary to obtain gauge). Begin at arrow for your size and rep pattern around. Continue working pattern following Chart **III** for the rest of the body.

Note: The 2 sts at each side of each side marker should always be purled with Color 2.

Shaping Sides: Continue as est until body measures a total of 13½ (13¾, 13¾, 14¼, 14¼) in / 34 (35, 35, 36, 36) cm. Now decrease 2 sts at each side, on every 4th rnd, 18 (19, 20, 18, 18) times. Decrease as follows: Knit until 2 sts before the 2 purl sts at side, k2tog tbl, p2, k2tog. Decrease the same way at opposite side. After completing decreases, 209 (223, 239, 263, 291) sts rem. Continue without further shaping until body measures a total of 24½ (24¾, 25¼, 25½, 26) in / 62 (63, 64, 65, 66) cm.

Side Increases: Now increase at each side as follows: Knit until 2 sts before side sts, increase 1, p2, increase 1. Work new sts into pattern. Increase the same way on every other rnd a total of 5 (5, 5, 4, 4) times = 219 (233, 249, 271, 299) sts. There should now be 111 (119, 129, 143, 157) pattern sts on the back and 1 purl st at each side and 52 (56, 60, 68, 75) sts for each front plus 1 purl st at side = 106 (114,

122, 138, 152) front sts total + 6 steek sts. Continue working in the round until body measures a total of 29¼ (29½, 30, 30¼, 30¾) in / 74 (75, 76, 77, 78) cm.

Shape Armholes: When 4 sts before side st, BO 10 sts, knit until 4 sts before opposite side marker and BO 10 sts, knit to end of rnd. On the next rnd, CO 6 sts over each gap for side steeks. Always purl steek sts and remember they are not included in stitch counts. Continue in the round. On every other rnd, at each side of front and back (on each side of side steeks), decrease 1 st 5 times and, on every 4th rnd, decrease 1 st 3 times. Continue in pattern.

Neck Shaping: When 3¼ in / 8 cm before total length, shape center front neck and begin working back and forth in pattern. BO the 6 steek sts + 10 (11, 11, 12, 13) sts at each side of steek. Then, on every other row, BO 2 sts 1 time and 1 st 5 (5, 6, 6, 6) times. Work as est until body is 37 (37¾, 38½, 39½, 40¼) in / 94 (96, 98, 100, 102) cm long. BO rem sts for shoulder on each side.

Back: Work as for front but begin neck shaping when 1¼ in / 3 cm from total length. BO the center back 37 (39, 41, 43, 45) sts. At neck edge, on every other row, BO another 1 st 2 times. BO rem sts for shoulder.

SLEEVES
With U. S. 2.5 / 3 mm dpn and Color 1, CO 65 (65, 70, 70, 75) sts. Divide sts onto dpn and join. Work around in p2, k3 ribbing) for 3½ in / 9 cm. Continuing with ribbing, and, on every 5th rnd, increase 2 sts at center of underarm (on each side of center st) until there are 95 (99, 103, 107, 111) sts. Work new sts into ribbing. After completing increases, work without further shaping until sleeve is 19¼ (19¾, 19¾, 20, 20) in / 49 (50, 50, 51, 51) cm long. On the next rnd, BO 5 sts, work around until 6 sts rem and BO rem 6 sts (make sure the 11 sts bound off are centered on underarm). Now work back and forth. At each side of sleeve, on every other row, BO 2 sts 2 times and 1 st 5 times. Then, on every 4th row, BO 1 st 4 (4, 5, 5, 6) times. Work 4 rows and then BO 4 sts at beginning of each of the next 8 (8, 8, 10, 10) rows. BO rem sts. Set sleeve aside while you knit second sleeve the same way.

CHART I

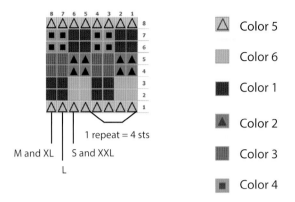

Color 5

Color 6

Color 1

Color 2

Color 3

Color 4

1 repeat = 4 sts

M and XL   S and XXL

L

CHART II

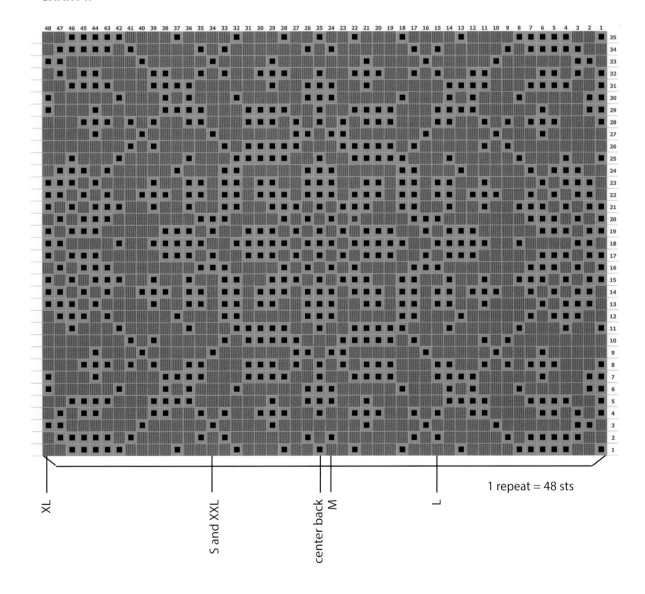

1 repeat = 48 sts

XL

S and XXL

center back

M

L

FINISHING

Weave in all ends neatly on WS. Gently steam press jacket on WS, under a damp pressing cloth. Seam shoulders.

Reinforce each steek by machine-stitching 2 zigzag lines on each side of center steek st. Carefully cut steek open up center st. Attach sleeves, leaving 2 in / 5 cm opening on each side of shoulder seam; ease in the extra width and sew in rest of sleeve.

Front Bands: With crochet hook and Color 3, beginning at lower edge of right front, work sc up to neck along right front (fold cut edges in and crochet along folded edge), Change to Color 2, turn, and work 1 row sc back down to bottom edge. Turn and sc up to neck.

Right Front Band with Buttonholes: Mark spacing for 7 buttonholes, evenly spaced on right front band, with the top one 2 sc below top edge and bottom one 15¾ in / 40 cm above lower edge. Turn and work 1 row sc, making buttonholes at the same time: for each buttonhole, ch 4, skip 3 sc, sc into next sc and each sc to next buttonhole.

After buttonhole row, turn and work 1 more row sc, with 3 sc in each ch loop. Turn and work 1 more row sc. Change to Color 3 and work 1 row sc. Cut yarn and fasten off. Weave in all ends neatly on WS.

Left Front Band: Work as for right band, omitting buttonholes.

Neckband: With crochet hook and Color 3, begin at right front band. Work 1 row sc along neckline, ending at left front band. Change to Color 2; turn and work 4 rows sc. Change to Color 3 and work 1 row sc. Cut yarn and fasten off. Weave in all ends neatly on WS.

Sew buttons to left front band to match buttonholes. Hand-stitch ribbon to WS of each front band to cover cut edges.

CHART III

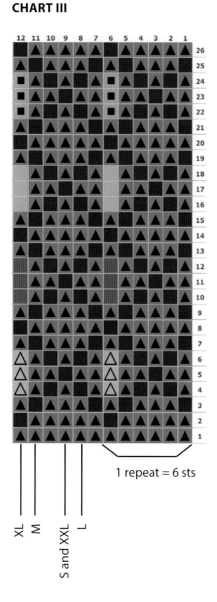

1 repeat = 6 sts

XL
M
S and XXL
L

△ Color 5

Color 6

Color 1

▲ Color 2

Color 3

Color 4

JOYOUS LILIES

This shaped jacket has lace edges. You can't help but feel anything other than joy when seeing lilies dance with lovely lace knitting and rolled edges. This jacket has slight waist shaping and is framed with rolled edges in tone-on-tone colors. It's knitted in a pretty tweed yarn in several shades that "fade" within the body of the jacket.

SKILL LEVEL
Experienced

SIZES
S (M, L, XL)

FINISHED MEASUREMENTS
Chest: approx. 36¼ (37, 41, 46) in / 92 (94, 104, 117) cm
Total Length: approx. 22¾ (23¾, 24½, 25¼) in / 58 (60, 62, 64) cm
Sleeve Length: approx. 19¼ (19¾, 19¾, 19¾) in / 49 (50, 50, 50) cm

YARN
CYCA #1 (fingering) Brooklyn Tweed Loft (100% Targhee-Columbia wool, 275 yd/251 m / 50 g)

YARN COLORS AND AMOUNTS
Color 1: Hayloft 112 (ochre): 100 (100, 100, 100) g
Color 2: Bale 136 (light yellow): 200 (200, 300, 300) g
Color 3: Fossil 101 (natural): 200 (200, 300, 300) g

SUGGESTED NEEDLE SIZES
U. S. sizes 4 (6) / 3.5 (4): circulars and sets of dpn; cable needle.
You may want to use U. S. 6 / 4 mm needles for the stranded colorwork.

CROCHET HOOK
U. S. size B-1/C-2 / 2.5 mm

NOTIONS
6 buttons to match jacket
Approx. 47¼ in / 120 cm long, ⅝ in / 1.5 cm wide ribbon to cover cut edges of steek behind front bands

GAUGE
24 sts in pattern on U. S. 4 (6) / 3.5 (4) mm needles = 4 in / 10 cm.
Adjust needle size to obtain correct gauge if necessary.

BODY

Lace Edging on Lower Body: Worked back and forth. With U. S. 4 / 3.5 mm circular and Color 1, CO 257 (274, 291, 325) sts. Knit 4 rows = garter edge. Now work in pattern following Chart **II**. Work 15 (16, 17, 19) reps across, ending p2. Work 1 rep in length. On Row 19 of chart, each rep has a double decrease = 227 (242, 257, 287) sts rem. On the last row (WS), decrease 4 (5, 6, 6) sts evenly spaced across = 223 (237, 251, 281) sts. Set piece aside.

Rolled Edge: Worked back and forth. With U. S. 4 / 3.5 mm circular and Color 2, CO 223 (237, 251, 281) sts. Work 8 rows in stockinette. Set piece aside.

Joining Edgings: Hold rolled edge over lace edging and join the pieces with Color 3. K2tog with 1 st each from lace and rolled edgings = 223 (237, 251, 281) sts. CO 6 new sts at end of row = center front steek. Now join to work in the round and knit 1 rnd.

Place Markers: Count 6 steek sts at center front pm; count 46 (50, 54, 60) sts, pm = right front; count 17 sts = side sts, pm at center of side sts and pm after side sts. Count 97 (103, 109, 127) sts = back, pm; count 17 sts = side sts, pm at center of side sts and pm after side sts. Count 46 (50, 54, 60) sts, pm = left front.

CHART I

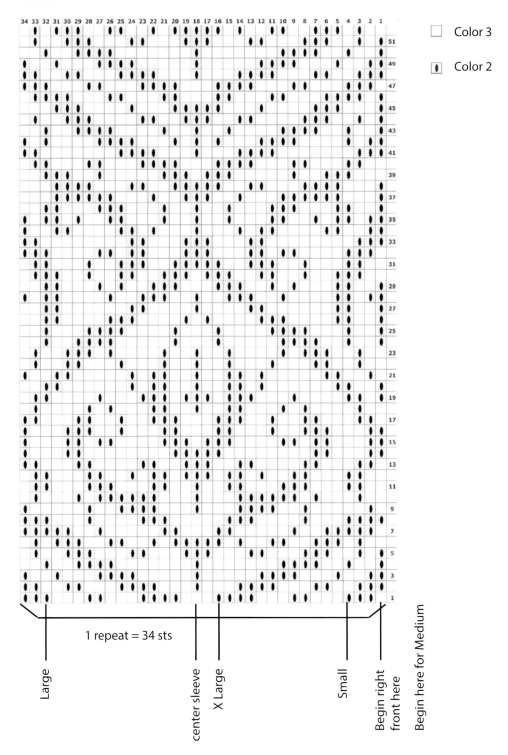

1 repeat = 34 sts

Large

center sleeve

X Large

Small

Begin right front here

Begin here for Medium

☐ Color 3

◖ Color 2

CHART II

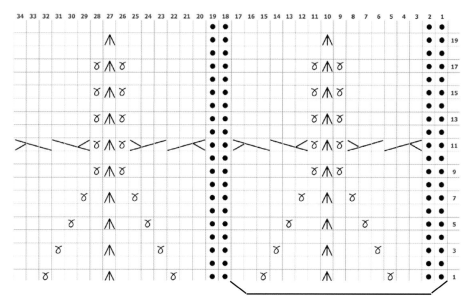

1 repeat = 17 sts; after the decreases on
Row 19, 1 repeat = 15 sts

⊡	Purl on RS, knit on WS
☐	Knit on RS, purl on WS
Ꝺ	K1tbl
⋀	Sl 1, k2tog, psso = 2 sts decreased
⊳─┬─┬─⊲	Place 3 sts on cable needle and hold in back of work, k3, k3 from cable needle
⊳─┴─┴─⊲	Place 3 sts on cable needle and hold in front of work, k3, k3 from cable needle

Pattern: The pattern is worked on a U. S. 4 or 6 / 3.5 or 4 mm circular (depending on which gives you the correct gauge) with a stripe pattern at the sides. Work in charted colorwork pattern on right front. See arrow on chart for beginning point for your size. Work stripe pattern: *k1 in Color 2, k1 in Color 3*; rep * to * over side sts, ending with k1 in Color 2.

Work in pattern over back, beginning at arrow for your size. Work stripe pattern: *k1 in Color 2, k1 in Color 3*; rep * to * over side sts, ending with k1 in Color 3. Work the left front mirror-image to match right front.

Note: Always purl the 6 steek sts with Color 1.

Work as est until body measures a total of 4¼ (4¾, 5¼, 5½) in / 11 (12, 13, 14) cm. Now decrease 2 sts at each side: Knit until 1 st before center st of right side

panel, sl 1, k2tog, psso. Decrease the same way on left side panel. Decrease the same way at each side on every 3rd rnd a total of 6 times = 199 (213, 227, 257) sts + 6 steek sts rem. Continue in pattern as est until body measures a total of 7½ (8, 8¼, 8¾) in / 19 (20, 21, 22) cm. Now increase 1 st on each side of markers on side panels on every 4th rnd 4 times = 215 (229, 243, 273) sts + 6 steek sts. Continue in pattern as est until body measures a total of 14½ (15, 15½, 15¾) in / 37 (38, 39, 40) cm.

Shape Armholes: Knit until 5 sts rem before side marker, BO 9 sts, knit until 5 sts before opposite side marker, BO 9 sts and knit to end of rnd. On the next rnd, CO 6 sts at each side over the gaps for the armhole steeks. Always purl these 6 steek sts with Color 3; steek sts are not included in st counts. Continue working around.

Further Armhole Shaping on Front and Back: At each side, on front and back armhole edges, on every other rnd, BO 2 sts 2 times and 1 st 4 times. BO just before/after steek sts.

At the same time, when 4¼ in / 11 cm before total length, shape front neck and begin working back and forth. BO the center front 22 sts + 6 steek sts for front neck. Then, at each side, at neck edge on every

other row, BO 2 sts 4 times and 1 st 5 (5, 6, 6) times. Continue until body measures 22¾ (23¾, 24½, 25¼) in / 58 (60, 62, 64) cm. BO all rem sts.

SLEEVES

Lace Edging on Sleeve: Worked back and forth. With U. S. 4 / 3.5 mm circular and Color 1, CO 70 sts (all sizes). Knit 4 rows = garter edge. Now work in pattern following Chart **II**. Work 4 reps across, ending p2. Work 1 rep in length. On Row 19 of chart, each rep has a double decrease = 62 sts rem. Set piece aside.

Rolled Edge: Worked back and forth. With U. S. 4 / 3.5 mm circular and Color 2, CO 62 sts. Work 8 rows in stockinette. Set piece aside.

Joining Edgings: Hold rolled edge over lace edging and join the pieces with Color 3. K2tog with 1 st each from lace and rolled edgings = 62 sts. Now divide sts onto dpn and join to work in the round and knit 1 rnd, and, *at the same time*, increase 3 (5, 7, 9) sts evenly spaced around = 65 (67, 69, 71) sts.

Now work in pattern following Chart I. See arrow for center of sleeve and count out to determine where to begin sleeve for your size. On every 6th rnd, increase 2 sts centered on underarm until there are 87 (91, 95, 103) sts. Continue as est without further shaping until sleeve is 19¼ (19¾, 19¾, 19¾) in / 49 (50, 50, 50) cm long.

Shape Armholes: On the next rnd, BO 5 sts, knit until 5 sts rem and BO 5 sts. Now begin working back and forth. At each side of sleeve, on every other row, BO 2 sts 2 times and 1 st 5 times. Now, on every 4th row, BO 1 st 5 (5, 6, 6) times. Work 6 rows and then BO 6 sts each at beginning of next 8 (8, 10, 10) rows. BO rem sts. Set sleeve aside while you knit second sleeve the same way.

Sleeve Facings: With U. S. 4 / 3.5 mm dpn or short circular and Color 2, with WS facing, pick up approx. 120 (126, 132, 144) sts around sleeve cap. Work 1 rnd knit tbl and then work 5 rnds in stockinette. BO loosely. Work facing on second sleeve the same way.

FINISHING

Weave in all ends neatly on WS. Gently steam press sweater on WS under a damp pressing cloth. Reinforce each steek by machine-stitching with 2 zigzag lines on each side of center steek st. Carefully cut open each steek up center st. Seam shoulders.

Neckband: The neckband is made with 3 rolled edges.

1st Rolled Edge, with Color 1: With U. S. 4 / 3.5 mm needle, pick up and knit 49 (50, 51, 52) sts along neck bind-off of right front, 48 (50, 52, 54) sts on back neck, and 49 (50, 51, 52) sts along neck bind-off of left front. Work 1 row knit tbl. Work 11 rows stockinette, knit 1 row on WS. BO and, *at the same time*, decrease 1 st at each shoulder and 1 st at beginning and end of neck edge on every other row on RS as follows: Pm at neck edge at each shoulder seam; k1, k2tog tbl, knit until 2 sts rem before marker at right shoulder; k2tog tbl, k2tog, knit until 2 sts before next marker; k2tog tbl, k2tog, knit until 3 sts rem and k2tog, k1.

2nd Rolled Edge, with Color 2: With U. S. 4 / 3.5 mm needle, pick up sts along back of 1st rolled edge, 1 st in each st. Work as for 1st rolled edge, but with 13 rows of stockinette, knit 1 row on WS and then BO.

3rd Rolled Edge, with Color 3: With U. S. 4 / 3.5 mm needle, pick up sts along back of 2nd rolled edge, 1 st in each st. Work as for 1st rolled edge.

Crocheted Left Front Band: With crochet hook and Color 2, work 1 row sc along left front edge, beginning where pattern begins and up to neckline. Turn and work 1 row sc down front. Change to Color 1 and work 2 rows sc. Change to Color 3 and work 2 rows sc + 1 row crab st (= sc worked from left to right). Cut yarn and fasten off securely.

Crocheted Right Front Band: Mark placement for 6 buttons on left band with bottom button 2 sc above bottom edge and top one ¼ in / 0.5 cm from top edge. Work right band as for left band, but, on 3rd row, make buttonholes: Ch 4, skip 3 sc and work 1 sc in next sc. On next row, work 3 sc in each ch loop.

Crochet Tip: Work 1 sc in each 5th row, skip 1 row. That will make the crocheted edge firmer.

Sew on buttons to match buttonholes. Attach sleeves. Fold facing over cut steek edge on each sleeve and sew down smoothly. Gently steam press sweater on WS under damp pressing cloth. Let rolled edges at neck roll in smoothly.

NIGHT LILY

This pullover makes me think of baroque wall hangings from castles and palaces in central Europe. The sweater's long ribbing drapes instead of pulling in; the large, pretty collar is quite wide and gives the sweater an elegant, feminine look. I chose a tweed yarn with shades of each color nuance to better pick up tones from other colors.

SKILL LEVEL
Experienced

SIZES
S (M, L, XL, XXL)

FINISHED MEASUREMENTS
Chest: approx. 41¾ (45, 48, 52, 56) in / 106 (114, 122, 132, 142) cm
Total Length: approx. 25¼ (25, 26¾, 27½, 28¼) in / 64 (66, 68, 70, 72) cm
Sleeve Length: approx. 19¼ (19¼, 19¾, 19¾, 20) in / 49 (49, 50, 50, 51) cm or desired length

YARN
CYCA #1 (fingering) Brooklyn Tweed Loft (100% Targhee-Columbia wool, 275 yd/251 m / 50 g)

YARN COLORS AND AMOUNTS
Color 1: Plume 125 (dark red violet): 300 (300, 400, 400, 400) g
Color 2: Homemade Jam 108 (dark red): 100 (100, 100, 200, 200) g
Color 3: Blanket Fort 126 (grey purple): 100 (200, 200, 200, 200) g

SUGGESTED NEEDLE SIZES
U. S. sizes 4 (6) / 3.5 (4): circulars and sets of dpn
You may want to use U. S. 6 / 4 mm needles for the stranded colorwork.

GAUGE
24 sts in stockinette/pattern on U. S. 4 (6) / 3.5 (4) mm needles = 4 in / 10 cm.
Adjust needle size to obtain correct gauge if necessary.

BODY
With U. S. 4 / 3.5 mm circular and Color 1, CO 420 (455, 490, 530, 570) sts. Join, being careful not to twist cast-on row; pm for beginning of rnd. Work around in p3, k2 ribbing for 3¼ in / 8 cm. Change to Color 2 and work in ribbing for ¾ in / 2 cm. On the next rnd, decrease as follows: *Sl 1, p2tog, psso, k2*; rep * to * around = 252 (273, 294, 318, 342) sts rem. Change to Color 1 and knit 2 rnds, but, on the 1st rnd, increase 2 (1, 0, 0, 0) sts evenly spaced around = 254 (274, 294, 318, 342) sts. Pm marker at each side = 127 (137, 147, 159, 171) sts on each side.

Pattern: Change to U. S. 6 / 4 mm needles if necessary for gauge and work in pattern following the chart. Begin at arrow for your size and work to side marker = front. Work back the same way.

When body is 15 (15½, 15¾, 15¾, 15¾) in / 38 (39, 40, 40, 40) cm long, divide for front and back at side markers. Now work front and back separately, back and forth.

Back: Work back and forth.

Shape Armholes: BO 2 sts each at beginning of next 8 rows. Continue in pattern as est until armhole depth is 8¾ (9, 9½, 10¼, 11) in / 22 (23, 24, 26, 28) cm. Next, bind off to shape neck and shoulders at the same time.

Neck Shaping: BO the center 31 (33, 35, 37, 39) sts for back neck. Work each side separately. At neck edge, on every other row, BO 2 sts 3 times.

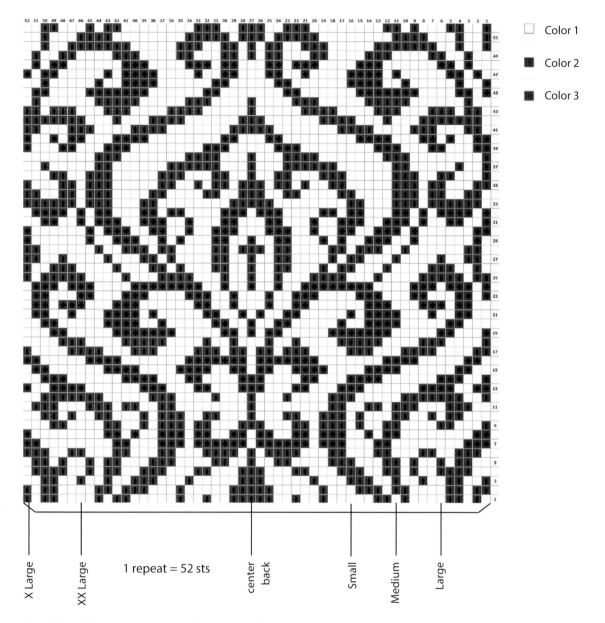

Color 1
Color 2
Color 3

X Large

XX Large

1 repeat = 52 sts

center back

Small

Medium

Large

Shoulder Shaping: On every other row, working from outer side of shoulder, BO 7-7-7-8 (8-8-8-8, 9-9-9-9, 10-10-10-10, 11-11-11-12) sts. No sts rem at shoulder. Work the other side to correspond.

Front: Work as for back but shape neck when 4 in / 10 cm before total length.

Neck Shaping: BO the center 27 (29, 31, 33, 35) sts for back neck. Work each side separately. At neck edge, on every other row, BO 2 sts 1 time and 1 st 6 times. Shape shoulder when at same length and the same way as for back. Work the other side to correspond.

SLEEVES

With U. S. 4 / 3.5 mm dpn and Color 1, CO 95 (100, 105, 110, 115) sts. Divide sts onto dpn and join; pm for beginning of rnd at center of underarm. Work around in p3, k2 ribbing for 3¼ in / 8 cm. Change to Color 2 and work in ribbing for ¾ in / 2 cm. On the next rnd, decrease as follows: *Sl 1, p2tog, psso, k2*; rep * to * around = 57 (60, 63, 66, 69) sts rem. Change to Color 1 and continue in stockinette.

Sleeve Shaping: Increase 1 st on each side of center underarm st on every 5th rnd until there are 103 (109, 115, 121, 129) sts. Continue straight up until sleeve is 19¼ (19¼, 19¾, 19¾, 20) in / 49 (49, 50,

50, 51) cm long or desired length. Divide sleeve in half at center of underarm and work back and forth in stockinette. BO 2 sts at beginning of each of next 8 rows and then BO rem sts loosely. Make the second sleeve the same way.

FINISHING
Seam shoulders.

Neckband: With U. S. 4 / 3.5 mm short circular and Color 1, pick up and knit 65 (67, 69, 71, 73) sts on front neck and 58 (59, 60, 61, 62) sts on back neck.

Work 1 rnd knit tbl and then work 6 rnds k2, p1 ribbing. Now increase 1 st in each purl st and work in k2, p2 ribbing until neckband is 3¼ in / 8 cm high. Next, increase 1 st in each purl column and work in k2, p3 ribbing until neckband is 8 in / 20 cm high. Change to Color 2 and work in ribbing for ¾ in / 2 cm. BO.

Attach sleeves. Weave in all ends neatly on WS. Gently steam press sweater on WS under damp pressing cloth.

✤ AUTUMN SERENADE

A few years ago, I created a photography series that I called "The Beauty of Death." I took pictures autumn leaves floating in water, hoping to capture the loveliness of a natural ending. This sweater-jacket was inspired by the colors in those photos. Autumn Serenade has a dress-like silhouette, with set-in sleeves and an A-line shaping. The front bands are crocheted in colors from the knitted pattern, and the jacket is topped off with a pretty collar.

SKILL LEVEL
Experienced

SIZES
S (M, L, XL, XXL)

FINISHED MEASUREMENTS
Chest: approx. 36 (38½, 41, 44½, 48¾) in / 91 (98, 104, 113, 124) cm
Circumference: at lower edge, approx. 44½ (47¾, 50¾, 55½, 60¼) in / 113 (121, 129, 141, 153) cm
Total Length: approx. 33 (34, 34¾, 35½, 36¼) in / 84 (86, 88, 90, 92) cm
Sleeve Length: approx. 19¼ (19¾, 19¾, 20, 20) in / 49 (50, 50, 51, 51) cm

YARN
CYCA #1 (fingering) Brooklyn Tweed Loft (100% Targhee-Columbia wool, 275 yd/251 m / 50 g)

YARN COLORS AND AMOUNTS
Color 1: Hayloft 112 (ochre): 300 (300, 300, 400, 400) g
Color 2: Old World 124 (dark blue): 100 (100, 200, 200, 200) g
Color 3: Thistle 107 (purple): 100 (100, 100, 100, 100) g
Color 4: Almanac 116 (petroleum): 100 (100, 100, 100, 100) g
Color 5: Flannel 137 (gray-blue): 100 (100, 100, 100, 100) g

SUGGESTED NEEDLE SIZES
U. S. sizes 4 (6) / 3.5 (4): circulars and sets of dpn

You may want to use U. S. 6 / 4 mm needles for the stranded colorwork.

CROCHET HOOK
U. S. size D-3 / 3 mm

NOTIONS
10 buttons to match jacket
Approx. 2¼ yd / 2 m ribbon to cover cut edges behind front bands

GAUGE
24 sts in pattern on U. S. 4 (6) / 3.5 (4) mm needles = 4 in / 10 cm.
24 sts in stockinette on U. S. 4 / 3.5 mm needles = 4 in / 10 cm.
Adjust needle sizes to obtain correct gauge if necessary.

Note: Read through the entire pattern before you begin knitting, as several steps are worked at the same time. Also, be sure to read the information on the charts. If you knit stranded colorwork tightly, go up a needle size and knit a swatch first to make sure your gauge is correct.

BODY

The body is knitted in the round with a steek (extra sts to be cut open when finishing) at center front. Always purl steek sts.

Ribbing at Lower Edge: With U. S. 4 / 3.5 mm circular and Color 1, CO 272 (292, 312, 342, 367)

CHART I

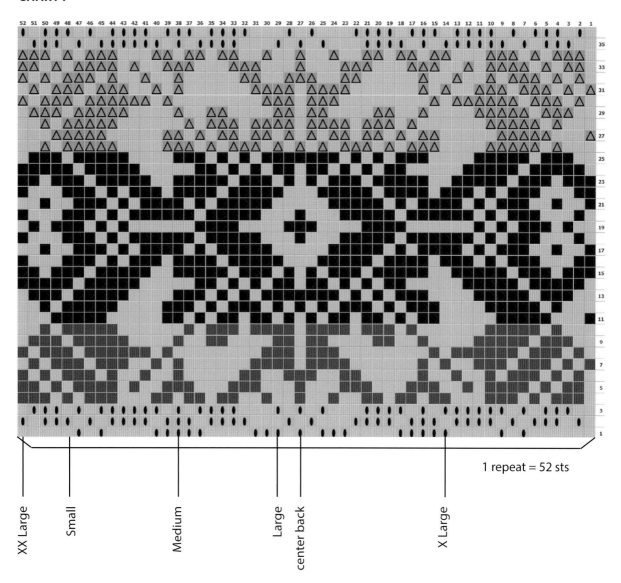

1 repeat = 52 sts

XX Large · Small · Medium · Large · center back · X Large

- (Color 5) Color 5
- (Color 1) Color 1
- (Color 3) Color 3
- (Color 2) Color 2
- (Color 4) Color 4

sts + 6 steek sts (steek sts are not included in stitch counts). Join, being careful not to twist cast-on row; pm for beginning of rnd. Work around in p2, k3 ribbing, ending with p2, for 3½ in / 9 cm. Knit 1 rnd, decreasing 1 (1, 3, 3, 0) sts evenly spaced around = 271 (291, 309, 339, 367) sts rem. Pm at each side with 66 (71, 76, 83, 90) sts for each side of front (not including the 6 steek sts) and 139 (149, 157, 173, 187) sts for back. Continue 2 purl sts up each side throughout.

Pattern Following Chart I: Work in pattern following Chart I, changing to U. S. 6 / 4 mm circular if necessary to obtain gauge. Begin at arrow for your size.

Decreases at Sides: Work straight up in pattern until body measures a total of 9½ (9¾, 9¾, 10¼, 10¼) in / 24 (25, 25, 26, 26) cm. Now decrease 2 sts at

CHART II

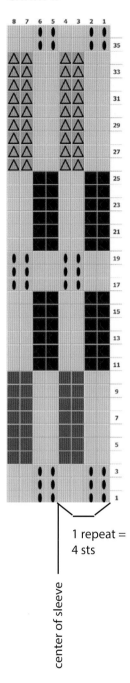

1 repeat =
4 sts

center of sleeve

⬛ Color 5

▦ Color 1

⬛ Color 3

⬛ Color 2

△ Color 4

each side, on every 4ᵗʰ rnd 18 (19, 20, 18, 18) times: Knit until 2 sts before the 2 purl side sts, k2tog tbl, p2, k2tog. Decrease the same way on opposite side. After completing decreases, 199 (215, 229, 267, 295) sts rem. Continue in pattern until body measures a total of 20½ (21, 21¼, 21¾, 22) in / 52 (53, 54, 55, 56) cm.

Increases at Sides: Now increase 2 sts at each side, on every other rnd 5 (5, 5, 4, 4) times: Knit to the 2 purl side sts, increase 1 st, p2, increase 1 st. Increase the same way on opposite side. Work new sts into pattern. After completing increases, 219 (235, 249, 283, 311) sts rem. There should now be 111 (119, 129, 143, 157) pattern sts on the back + 1 purl st at each side of back and 52 (56, 60, 68, 75) sts on each front + 1 purl side st = 106 (114, 122, 138, 152) total sts on front + 6 steek sts. Continue working in the round until body measures a total of 25¼ (25½, 26, 26½, 26¾) in / 64 (65, 66, 67, 68) cm.

Shape Armholes: Work until 4 sts rem before side sts, BO 10 sts. Knit until 4 sts before next side st, BO 10 sts and compete rnd. On the next rnd,

CO 6 sts at each side over the gap at each underarm = armhole steeks. Always purl these sts and do not include in st counts. Continue knitting in the round. Decrease at each side of steek on front and back on every other rnd 1 st 5 times and on every 4ᵗʰ rnd 1 st 3 times. Continue working in pattern as est.

Neck Shaping: When body is 3¼ in / 8 cm before total length, shape neck and work back and forth in pattern. BO the 6 center front steek sts and 10 (11, 11, 12, 13) sts on each side of steek. Next, on every other row, at neck edge, BO 2 sts 1 time and 1 st 5 (5, 6, 6, 6) times. Continue in pattern until body measures 33 (34, 34¾, 35½, 36¼) in / 84 (86, 88, 90, 92) cm. BO rem sts for shoulders.

Back: Work as for front but shape neck when 1¼ in / 3 cm before total length. BO the center 37 (39, 41, 43, 45) sts. On every other row, at neck edge, BO 1 st 2 times. BO rem sts for shoulders.

SLEEVES

With U. S. 4 / 3.5 mm dpn and Color 1, CO 65 (65, 70, 70, 75) sts. Divide sts onto dpn and join; pm for beginning of rnd at center of underarm. Work around in p2, k3 ribbing for 3½ in / 9 cm. Knit 1 rnd, increasing 1 st = 66 (66, 71, 71, 76) sts. Work around in pattern following Chart **II**, changing to U. S. 6 / 4 mm dpn if necessary to obtain gauge. See arrow for center of sleeve and count out to determine beginning st for your size.

Sleeve Shaping: Increase 1 st on each side of center underarm st *at the same time* as beginning pattern on every 5th rnd until there are 82 (86, 90, 94, 98) sts. Work new sts into pattern. Continue straight up until sleeve is 19¼ (19¾, 19¾, 20, 20) in / 49 (50, 50, 51, 51) cm long or desired length. Work next rnd as follows: BO 5 sts, knit until 5 sts rem, BO last 5 sts. Now work back and forth. On each side of sleeve on every other row, BO 2 sts 2 times and 1 st 5 times. Next, on every 4th row, BO 1 st 4 (4, 5, 5, 6) times. Work 4 rows and then BO 4 sts at beginning of each of next 8 (8, 8, 10, 10) rows and then BO rem sts loosely. Make the second sleeve the same way.

FINISHING

Seam shoulders. Reinforce each steek by machine-stitching with 2 zigzag lines on each side of center steek st. Carefully cut open each steek up center st.

Crocheted Front Bands: Begin at lower edge of right front with crochet hook and Color 4. Fold cut edges to WS and work sc along foldline up to neck. Turn and work sc back down to lower edge. For buttonholes: Change to Color 2. Mark spacing for 10 buttonholes, with the top one 2 sc from top edge and the bottom one in row between ribbing and pattern at lower edge. Turn and work in sc, making each buttonhole as follows: ch 3, skip 2 sc, continue in sc to next buttonhole. On next row, change to Color 4, turn and work in sc, working 2 sc in each ch loop.

Turn and work a row in sc. Change to Color 1 and work 1 more row in sc. Cut yarn and fasten off securely.

Make left front button band as for right band, omitting buttonholes.

Collar: With U. S. 4 / 3.5 mm short circular and Color 1, pick up and knit 39 (40, 41, 43, 45) sts along right front neckline, 39 (42, 45, 46, 47) sts along back neck, and 39 (40, 41, 43, 45) sts along left front neckline. Work back in purl tbl. Now work back and forth in p3, k2 ribbing, ending with p2 for 4¼ in / 11 cm. BO in ribbing. Cut yarn and fasten off securely.

Sew buttons onto left front band to match buttonholes. Hand-stitch ribbon to back of each front band to cover cut steek edges. Attach sleeves, leaving 2 in / 5 cm open on each side of each shoulder seam. Ease in sleeve top and finish seam. Weave in all ends neatly on WS. Gently steam press sweater on WS under damp pressing cloth.

MEN'S SNOWTRACK PULLOVER

This sweater was inspired by an old mitten I found displayed in the DigitalMuseum. At first glance, the pattern looked like a traditional Selbu design. However, it differed from that tradition by mixing several traditional characteristics, as, for example, the vertical bands that separate the front and back. The mitten was embellished with a large centered star motif surrounded by a simple overall pattern. My idea was to take a traditional Icelander sweater with its characteristic simple overall patterning as a starting point, and to transfer the pretty mitten motif to the sweater. The result was a new twist on the traditional Icelander with large "mitten roses" on the yoke and bands to separate the different sections to make the raglan particularly noticeable and stylish.

SKILL LEVEL
Experienced

SIZES
XS (S, M, L, XL, XXL)

FINISHED MEASUREMENTS
Chest: approx. 35½ (39½, 43¼, 47¼, 51¼, 55¼) in / 90 (100, 110, 120, 130, 140) cm
Total Length: approx. 23¾ (24¾, 25½, 26¾, 27¼, 28¼) in / 60 (63, 65, 68, 69, 72) cm
Sleeve Length: approx. 20 (20½, 20½, 21, 21¼, 21¾) in / 51 (52, 52, 53, 54, 55) cm

YARN
CYCA #2 (sport, baby) Rauma Finull PT2 (100% Norwegian wool, 191 yd/175 m / 50 g)

YARN COLORS AND AMOUNTS
Natural White 401: 300 (300, 400, 400, 450, 500) g
Black 436: 350 (400, 400, 450, 450, 500) g

SUGGESTED NEEDLE SIZES
U. S. sizes 1.5 and 2.5 / 2.5 and 3 mm: circulars and sets of 5 dpn.

Note: If you knit stranded colorwork more firmly than single-color knitting, you should go up a needle size.

GAUGE
26 sts in pattern on larger needles = 4 in / 10 cm. Adjust needle sizes to obtain correct gauge if necessary.

BODY

With Black and smaller circular, CO 214 (242, 266, 290, 318, 342) sts. Join, being careful not to twist cast-on row; pm for beginning of rnd). Work 20 rnds k1, p1 ribbing.
Change to larger circular and Natural White. Knit 1 rnd, *at the same time* increasing 22 sts evenly spaced around = 236 (264, 288, 312, 340, 364) sts around or 118 (132, 144, 156, 170, 182) sts each for front and back. Begin front and back each with Chart **B** and work the rest of the body following Chart **A**. Begin on 6th (6th, 5th, 5th, 5th, 4th, 4th) st of chart, so 2nd st of chart will be centered on front and back. Work following Charts **A** and **B** until body measures 16½ (17, 17¼, 18¼, 18½, 19) in / 42 (43, 44, 46, 47, 48) cm. On the last rnd, BO or place on holders 11 (11, 13, 15, 15, 17) sts centered at each underarm = 214 (242, 262, 282, 310, 330) sts rem. Set body aside while you knit sleeves.

SLEEVES

With Black and smaller dpn, CO 56 (58, 58, 60, 60, 62) sts. Divide sts onto dpn and join; pm for beginning of rnd. Work 20 rnds k1, p1 ribbing. Change to larger dpn and knit 1 rnd. With Natural White,

56

knit 1 rnd, increasing 4 sts evenly spaced around = 60 (62, 62, 64, 64, 66) sts. Begin sleeve following Chart **B**, centered on underarm. For the rest of the sleeve, work following Chart **A**, beginning with 5th (4th, 4th, 3rd, 3rd, 2nd) st of chart, so 2nd st of chart will be centered on sleeve. Work following Charts **A** and **B**, increasing on approx. every 4th rnd until there are a total of 108 (110, 114, 118, 122, 130) sts and sleeve is 20 (20½, 20½, 21, 21¼, 21¾) in / 51 (52, 52, 53, 54, 55) cm long. BO or place on holders the center 11 (11, 13, 15, 15, 17) sts on underarm.

97 (99, 101, 103, 107, 113) sts rem. Make sure you end on the same pattern row as for body when ending each sleeve. Set first sleeve aside while you knit second sleeve the same way.

YOKE: JOINING BODY AND SLEEVES/ RAGLAN SHAPING

Now it's time to join the body and sleeves on larger circular: front, sleeve, back, sleeve = total of 408 (440, 464, 488, 524, 556) sts. To ensure that the sts of Chart **B** are divided evenly between the pieces (front, back, and sleeves), k2tog with the two last sts of front and back and sleeves following Chart **B**. CO a new st between the pieces to work as 3rd st of Chart **B** before the next two sts on front and back and sleeves are worked following Chart **B** = a total of 5 sts following Chart **B**, centered on the band between pieces. The rest of the yoke is worked following Chart **C**.

Note: The pattern will not work out evenly around—it's broken after Chart **B** and adapted to the decreases.

Begin on 92nd (85th, 80th, 75th, 68th, 63rd) st on Chart **C**, so the st outlined in red on the chart (49th st) is centered on front and back. Correspondingly, for sleeves, begin on 1st (96th, 95th, 94th, 92nd, 89th) st on Chart **C**, so the st outlined in red on the chart

(49th st) is centered on both sleeves. Work 4 (8, 8, 8, 10, 12) rnds without decreasing. Next, begin raglan shaping.

Raglan Shaping: Always decrease with Natural White as follows: Knit until 2 sts before first band. K2tog with Natural White. Knit band following Chart **B**. Decrease on the other side of band with sl 1, k1 with Natural White, psso. You will decrease at different rates on the body and sleeves. On the sleeves, decrease on every 4th rnd 4 times, on every other rnd 8 times, and then on every rnd 19 (21, 23, 25, 27, 30) times. *At the same time*, on the front and back, decrease on every other rnd 16 times and on every rnd 19 (21, 23, 25, 27, 30) times. After all decreases, 128 (148, 160, 164, 196, 204) sts rem.

Neck Shaping: Work back and forth. At front, place the center 23 (25, 27, 29, 31, 35) sts on a holder. While you knit back and forth in pattern from Chart **A**, place 8,6,4,2 (8,6,4,2,2; 8,6,4,2,2,2; 8,6,4,4,2,2,2,2; 8,6,4,4,2,2,2,2; 8,6,4,4,2,2,2,2,2) sts on a holder for front neck. *At the same time*, continue shaping raglan on every row on each side of each band as before. On the last row, knit 1 row with Natural White counting sts as you knit. The total st count rem for neckband is 112 (120, 120, 128, 132, 132).

Change to smaller circular or use larger needle if you want a looser neckband, or omit last decrease row so the st count is higher. With Black, work around in k1, p1 ribbing for 5½ (5½, 6¼, 6¼, 7, 7) in / 14 (14, 16, 16, 18, 18) cm for a high neck. BO loosely in ribbing.

FINISHING

Seam underarms. Weave in all ends neatly on WS. Gently steam press sweater under a damp pressing cloth. Fold neck down to double it.

CHART A

CHART B

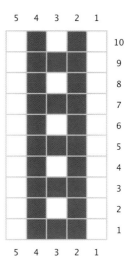

CHART C

☐ Natural White 401

■ Black 436

☐ Center st

ROYAL STAG MITTENS

These Royal Stag mittens are designed in the Selbu tradition, with characteristic shaping of the cuffs, thumb gusset, front decreases, and more. Animal motifs are found on many traditional mittens. Here, two stag heads are mirror-imaged towards each other to create a new pattern and an exciting overall design.

WOMEN'S MITTENS

SKILL LEVEL
Experienced

SIZE
Women's

FINISHED MEASUREMENTS
Circumference: approx. 8 in / 20.5 cm
Total Length: approx. 9 in / 23 cm

YARN
CYCA #1 (fingering) Rauma 2-ply Gammelserie
(100% Norwegian wool, 175 yd/160 m / 50 g)

YARN COLORS AND AMOUNTS
White GL400: 50 g
Dark Brown GL422: 50 g

SUGGESTED NEEDLE SIZES
U. S. size 0 / 2 mm: set of 5 dpn.

GAUGE
28 sts in stockinette = 4 in / 10 cm.
Adjust needle size to obtain correct gauge if necessary.

CUFF
You can choose to make a narrow or (wide) version of the cuff. With White and dpn, CO 56 (64) sts. Divide sts onto 4 dpn and join. Purl 1 rnd. Work the lace pattern as follows:
Rnd 1: *P1, k2tog, k4 (5), yo, k1, yo, k4 (5), k2tog*; rep * to * around.

Rnd 2: Work knit over knit and yarnovers, and purl over purl around.
Rep Rnds 1-2 for a total of 26 rnds. End with knit 1 rnd, adjusting st count to 57 (57).

MITTEN HAND
Continue, following **hand** chart, increasing for thumb gusset as shown on chart. At the red line above gusset on the chart, knit those sts with smooth, contrast color scrap yarn, which you will later remove. Slide the sts back to left needle and knit in pattern. Alternatively, you can place the thumb sts on a holder and CO the same number of sts over the gap. Continue to top shaping, paying attention to the decreases (use ssk or k2tog tbl) at the side of the thumb just after the gusset is complete. To shape top, decrease with ssk or sl 1, k1, psso for left-leaning decreases at beginning of Ndls 1 and 3; and with k2tog for right-leaning decreases at end of Ndls 2 and 4. After completing charted rows, cut yarn and draw through rem sts; tighten.

THUMB
Insert a dpn through 13 sts below scrap yarn and another dpn through 13 sts above scrap yarn. Carefully remove scrap yarn. Or, knit live held sts and pick up and knit same number of sts along cast-on row of thumbhole. To avoid holes, pick up and knit 1 extra st at each corner = 28 sts for thumb. Work following **thumb** chart. Shape and finish top as for top of mitten.

Weave in all ends neatly on WS. Make left-hand mitten the same way, but **don't** forget to place left thumb on left side of palm!

HAND

White GL400

Dark Brown GL422

Ssk or k2tog tbl

K2tog

scrap yarn

LLI

RLI

No stitch

THUMB

HAND

CUFF

THUMB

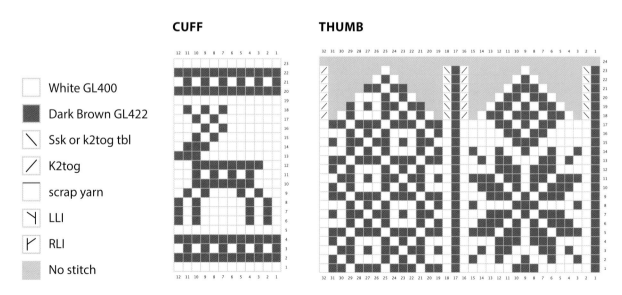

White GL400

Dark Brown GL422

Ssk or k2tog tbl

K2tog

scrap yarn

LLI

RLI

No stitch

MEN'S MITTENS

SIZE
Men's

FINISHED MEASUREMENTS
Circumference: approx. 9½ in / 24 cm
Total Length: approx. 11½ in / 29 cm

YARN
CYCA #1 (fingering) Rauma 2-ply Gammelserie
(100% Norwegian wool, 175 yd/160 m / 50 g)

YARN COLORS AND AMOUNTS
White GL400: 50 g
Dark Brown GL422: 50 g

SUGGESTED NEEDLE SIZES
U. S. size 0 and 1.5 / 2 and 2.5 mm: sets of 5 dpn.

GAUGE
28 sts in stockinette on larger needles = 4 in / 10 cm.
Adjust needle sizes to obtain correct gauge if
necessary.

CAST-ON
With smaller dpn and Natural White, CO 56 sts.
Divide sts onto 4 dpn and join. Work 4 rnds, k1tbl,
p1 ribbing. Change to larger dpn and knit 1 rnd, increasing 4 sts evenly spaced around = 60 sts.

CUFF and HAND
Work following **cuff** and then **hand** chart, increasing for thumb gusset as shown on chart. At the
red line above gusset on the chart, knit those sts
with smooth, contrast color scrap yarn, which you
will later remove. Slide the sts back to left needle
and knit in pattern. Alternately, you can place the
thumb sts on a holder and CO the same number of
sts over the gap. Continue to top shaping, noting
the decreases (use ssk or k2tog tbl) at the side of the
thumb just after the gusset is complete. To shape
top, decrease with ssk or sl 1, k1, psso for left-leaning
decreases at beginning of needles 1 and 3 and with
k2tog for right-leaning decreases at end of needles 2
and 4. After completing charted rows, cut yarn and
draw through rem sts; tighten.

THUMB
Insert a dpn through 15 sts below scrap yarn and
another dpn through 15 sts above scrap yarn. Carefully remove scrap yarn. Or, knit live held sts and
pick up and knit same number of sts along cast-on
row of thumbhole. To avoid holes, pick up and knit
1 extra st at each corner = 32 sts for thumb. Work
following **thumb** chart. Shape and finish top as for
top of mitten.

Weave in all ends neatly on WS. Make left-hand
mit-ten the same way, but don't forget to place left
thumb on left side of palm!

FANCY HAT

Norwegian traditional knitting is often worked with natural white and sheep's black wool yarn. Garments could be dyed red or other colors after they were knitted because that made them extra special. For example, this was traditional for many mittens gifted by brides in Selbu and for stockings in the Sunnfjord folk costume. This fancy hat features a traditional Selbu rose pattern in which the main and pattern colors change places in an "endless pattern" that can be repeated over a large surface. The shaping at the top is worked into the pattern for an elegant finish.

SKILL LEVEL
Experienced

SIZE
One size (can be adjusted by changing gauge, if desired)

FINISHED MEASUREMENTS
Circumference: approx. 23¾ in / 60 cm
Total Length: approx. 11½ in / 29 cm; with brim folded up, 9 in / 23 cm

YARN
CYCA #1 (fingering) Hillesvåg Vilje lamullgarn (100% Norwegian lamb's wool, 410 yd/375 m / 100 g)

YARN COLORS AND AMOUNTS
White 400: 100 g
Charcoal 415: 100 g

SUGGESTED NEEDLE SIZES
U. S. sizes 1.5 and 2.5 / 2.5 and 3 mm: short circulars and sets of 5 dpn.
For a smaller size, you can try going down half a needle size, but make sure to recheck your gauge on the new size!

GAUGE
25 sts in stockinette on larger needles = 4 in / 10 cm. Adjust needle size to obtain correct gauge if necessary.

With smaller circular or dpn and Charcoal, CO 132 sts. Join, being careful not to twist cast-on row; pm for beginning of rnd. Work 20 rnds in k2, p2 ribbing. Next, work 3 rnds p2, k2 ribbing for the foldline. Change to larger circular (change to dpn when sts no longer fit around circular).

Knit 1 rnd, increasing 12 sts evenly spaced around = 144 sts. Work following chart to the first decrease rnd. Decrease to shape crown as shown.

CROWN DECREASES
The decreases are worked into the pattern, with right- and left-leaning decreases as indicated on the chart. Work right-leaning decreases with k2tog and left-leaning with ssk or sl 1, k1, psso.

FINISHING
After completing charted rows, cut yarn and draw end through rem sts; tighten.
Weave in all ends neatly on WS. Gently steam press hat under a damp pressing cloth. Fold up brim at foldline.

☐ White 400
■ Charcoal 415
▨ No stitch
╱ Right-leaning decrease: k2tog
╲ Left-leaning decrease: ssk or sl 1, k1, psso

SNOWTRACK SOCKS

These Snowtrack socks were inspired by old "snowtrack" sweaters from Nordfjord, characterized by vertical stripes with simple motifs within the stripes. These socks use the same traditional motifs.

SKILL LEVEL
Experienced

SIZES
S (L)—Women's (Men's)

FINISHED MEASUREMENTS
Length of Leg: approx. 4¾ (6) in / 12 (15) cm
Length of Foot: as measured from heel, approx. 8¾ (10¼) in / 22 (26) cm

YARN
CYCA #1 (fingering) Trollkar Slitesterk (80% soft wool, 20% polyester, 383 yd/350 m / 100 g)

YARN COLORS AND AMOUNTS
Natural White 101: 100 (100) g
Charcoal Grey 995: 100 (100) g

SUGGESTED NEEDLE SIZES
U. S. sizes 0 and 1.5 / 2 and 2.5 mm: sets of 5 dpn.

Note: You can change the sock size by going up or down a needle size. If, for example, you want smaller socks, follow the chart for the Small size, using needles half a size smaller than recommended.

GAUGE
28 sts in stockinette on larger needles = 4 in / 10 cm. Adjust needle sizes to obtain correct gauge if necessary.

LEG
With smaller dpn and Natural White, CO 52 (72) sts. Divide sts onto 5 dpn and join. Work 4 rnds k1tbl, p1 ribbing. Knit 1 rnd, increasing 8 sts evenly spaced around = 60 (80) sts. Change to larger dpn and work in pattern following Chart A (B). Count out so

that the center st (outlined in red on the chart) is at the center of the sock leg. Work **A** (**B**) for 4¾ (6) in / 12 (15) cm or desired length for leg.

HEEL and GUSSET
Heel Flap: Work heel over 25 (33) sts between the side bands as on Chart **A** (**B**). Work back and forth in pattern for 24 (28) rows, always slipping the 1st st of each row purlwise. Each edge of the flap will have 12 (14) chain edge sts to make it easy to pick up sts later on.

Heel Turn: Work following Chart **C**, except for the center band of Chart **A** (**B**), which continues under the foot (see photo on page 71). The decreases for the heel turn occur at each side of this band. Work back and forth, beginning by knitting to end of band, k2tog, k1; turn. Sl 1, purl to opposite side of band, p2tog, p1; turn.
Row 1: Sl 1 purlwise, knit until 1 st before gap, k2tog, k1; turn.
Row 2: Sl 1 purlwise, purl until 1 st before gap, p2tog, p1; turn.
Rep Rows 1-2 until all sts have been worked.

Gusset: Pick up and knit 12 (14) sts on each side of heel flap, working across instep as est. On the next rnd, work heel flap sts as k1tbl to avoid holes.

Continue in the round in pattern, decreasing on every other rnd at each side, between Chart C for the sole and **A** (**B**) for the instep: Knit until 3 sts before instep, k2tog, k1; work across instep, k1, ssk, knit to end of rnd. *At the same time,* continue band down center of sole. When 60 (80) sts rem, continue in pattern as est until foot measures 7 (8) in / 18 (20) cm from heel or desired foot length before toe.

TOE

The toe is shaped on each side of side bands. The bands down center of sole and bands at each side of foot continue throughout, while the rest of the sts are worked following Chart **C**.

At the beginning of Ndls 1 and 3: Sl 1, k1, psso (or ssk).

At end of Ndls 2 and 4: K2tog.

CHART A

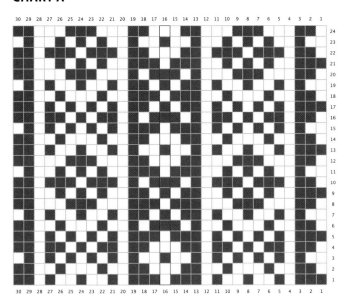

End toe decreases when no more sts rem between side bands. Either join bands with Kitchener st or cut yarn and draw through rem sts and tighten.

Make the second sock the same way.

FINISHING

Weave in all ends neatly on WS. Gently steam press socks under damp pressing cloth.

☐ Natural White 101
■ Charcoal Gray 995
☐ Center stitch

CHART B

CHART C

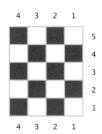

☐ Natural White 101
■ Charcoal Gray 995
☐ Center stitch

SPRUCE HAT AND COWL

People often think of winter as colorless. But, particularly in Vestlandet—where winter is often green—if you look closely, you'll see all kinds of different colors and shades. Spruce and evergreen forests are full of greens, browns, blue-grays, and grays: a beautiful palette.

HAT

SIZE
One size

FINISHED MEASUREMENTS
Circumference: approx. 22 in / 56 cm
Length: approx. 11 in / 28 cm

YARN
CYCA #2 (sport, baby) Rauma Finull PT2 (100% Norwegian wool, 191 yd/175 m / 50 g)

YARN COLORS AND AMOUNTS
Light Yellow Green 402: 50 g
Dark Brown 422: 50 g
Olive 476: 50 g

SUGGESTED NEEDLE SIZES
U. S. sizes 1.5 and 2.5 / 2.5 and 3 mm: short circular and set of 5 dpn

GAUGE
26 sts in stockinette on large size needles = 4 in / 10 cm
Adjust needle sizes to obtain correct gauge if necessary.

CAST-ON
With Dark Brown and smaller circular, CO 132 sts. Join, being careful not to twist cast-on row; pm for beginning of rnd. Work 3 rnds k1, p1 ribbing. Change to larger needle. Knit 1 rnd, increasing 12 sts evenly spaced around = 144 sts. Work around in pattern following Chart **A** (see page 75). After completing Chart **A**, continue with Dark Brown and stockinette until hat measures approx. 8 in / 20 cm or desired length before crown shaping. Change to dpn when sts no longer fit around circular.

CROWN SHAPING
Decrease Rnd 1: *K2tog, k6*; rep * to * around. Knit 6 rnds.
Decrease Rnd 2: *K2tog, k5*; rep * to * around. Knit 5 rnds.
Decrease Rnd 3: *K2tog, k4*; rep * to * around. Knit 4 rnds.
Decrease Rnd 4: *K2tog, k3*; rep * to * around. Knit 3 rnds.
Decrease Rnd 5: *K2tog, k2*; rep * to * around. Knit 2 rnds.
Decrease Rnd 6: *K2tog, k1*; rep * to * around. Knit 1 rnd.
Decrease Rnd 7: K2tog around.
Knit 1 rnd. Cut yarn and draw end through rem sts; tighten.

FINISHING
Weave in all ends neatly on WS. Gently steam press hat under damp pressing cloth.

COWL

SIZE
One size

FINISHED MEASUREMENTS
Circumference: approx. 22 in / 56 cm
Length: approx. 9¾ in / 25 cm

YARN
CYCA #2 (sport, baby) Rauma Finull PT2 (100% Norwegian wool, 191 yd/175 m / 50 g)

YARN COLORS AND AMOUNTS
Light Yellow Green 402: 50 g
Dark Brown 422: 50 g
Olive 476: 50 g

SUGGESTED NEEDLE SIZES
U. S. sizes 1.5 and 2.5 / 2.5 and 3 mm: 24 in / 60 cm circulars

GAUGE
26 sts in stockinette on large size needles =
4 in / 10 cm
Adjust needle sizes to obtain correct gauge if necessary.

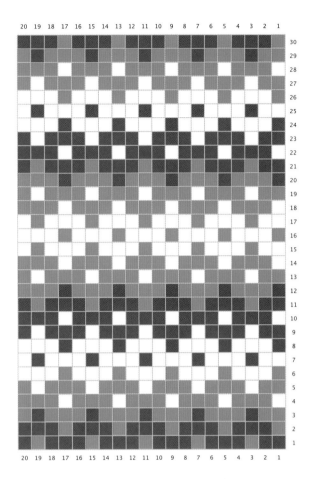

☐ 402 Light Yellow Green
■ 422 Dark Brown
■ 476 Olive

CAST-ON

With Dark Brown and smaller circular, CO 132 sts. Join, being careful not to twist cast-on row; pm for beginning of rnd. Work 3 rnds k1, p1 ribbing. Change to larger circular. Knit 1 rnd, increasing 12 sts evenly spaced around = 144 sts. Work around in pattern following Chart **A** until cowl is approx. 9 in / 23 cm high or desired length. Knit 1 rnd with Dark Brown and, *at the same time*, decrease 12 sts evenly spaced around = 132 sts. Change to smaller circular and work 3 rnds in k1, p1 ribbing. BO loosely.

FINISHING

Weave in all ends neatly on WS. Gently steam press cowl under damp pressing cloth.

✦ FIRDIR WOMEN'S PULLOVER

In the Nordfjord Folk Museum, you'll find several old "band sweaters," all distinguished by vertical stripes with narrow motifs within the stripes—all except one, which has a body and sleeves completely covered by a fascinating star pattern in multiple colors. The concept is further developed in this modern pullover, where the pattern is knitted only on the yoke for a more modern, dynamic look.

SKILL LEVEL
Experienced

SIZES
XS (S, M, L, XL, XXL)

FINISHED MEASUREMENTS
Chest: approx. 35½ (39½, 43¼, 47¼, 51¼, 55¼) in / 90 (100, 110, 120, 130, 140) cm
Total Length: approx. 22½ (23¼, 24, 24¾, 25¼, 26½) in / 57 (59, 61, 63, 64, 67) cm
Sleeve Length: approx. 19¾ (19¾, 20, 20, 20½, 20½) in / 50 (50, 51, 51, 52, 52) cm

YARN
CYCA #1 (fingering) Trollkar Supermjuk (Supersoft) (100% pure new wool, 383 yd/350 m / 100 g)

YARN COLORS AND AMOUNTS
Pine Needles 360: 300 (350, 400, 450, 500, 600) g
Light Gray 202: 200 (200, 200, 200, 200, 200) g

SUGGESTED NEEDLE SIZES
U. S. sizes 1.5 and 2.5 / 2.5 and 3 mm: circulars and sets of 5 dpn.

Note: If you knit stranded colorwork more firmly than single-color knitting, you should go up a needle size.

GAUGE
26 sts in stockinette on larger needles = 4 in / 10 cm. Adjust needle size to obtain correct gauge if necessary.

BODY
With Pine Needles and smaller circular, CO 214 (242, 266, 290, 318, 342) sts. Join, being careful not to twist cast-on row; pm for beginning of rnd). Work 20 rnds k1, p1 ribbing. Change to larger circular and knit 1 rnd. On the next rnd, increase 22 sts (all sizes) evenly spaced around = 236 (264, 288, 312, 340, 364) sts. Pm at each side with 118 (132, 144, 156, 170, 182) sts each for front and back. Always purl the last st at each side as a side st. Continue in stockinette until body measures 15½ (15½, 15¾, 16¼, 16½, 17) in / 39 (39, 40, 41, 42, 43) cm. On the last rnd, BO or place on holders 11 (11, 13, 15, 17, 17) sts centered at each underarm = 214 (242, 262, 282, 306, 330) sts. Set body aside while you knit the sleeves.

SLEEVES
With Pine Needles and smaller dpn, CO 54 (56, 56, 58, 58, 60) sts. Divide sts onto dpn and join; pm for beginning of rnd. Work 20 rnds k1, p1 ribbing. Change to larger dpn. Knit 1 rnd and, *at the same time*, increase 6 sts evenly spaced around (all sizes) = 60 (62, 62, 64, 64, 66) sts. Always purl the last st (center of underarm). Approx. every 5th rnd, increase 1 st on each side of the centered purl st until there are a total of 108 (110, 114, 118, 122, 130) sts. When sleeve is 19¾ (19¾, 20, 20, 20½, 20½) in / 50 (50, 51, 51, 52, 52) cm long or desired length, BO or place on holder the center 11 (11, 13, 15, 17, 17) sts on underarm = 97 (99, 101, 103, 105, 113) sts. Set first sleeve aside while you knit second sleeve the same way.

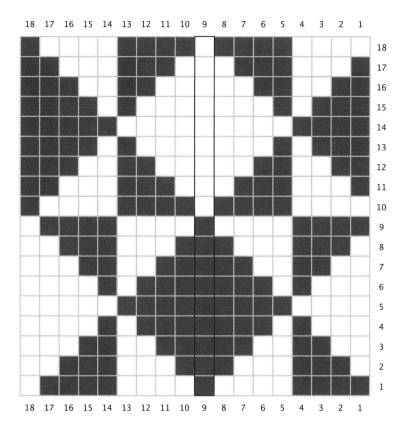

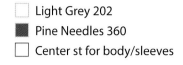

Light Grey 202
Pine Needles 360
Center st for body/sleeves

YOKE

Joining/Raglan Shaping

Note: Read through this entire section before you begin knitting.

Now it's time to join the body and sleeves on larger circular: front, sleeve, back, sleeve = 408 (440, 464, 488, 516, 556) sts. At each intersection of body and sleeve, pm and CO 1 st (purl this st throughout yoke; the purl st is not included in st counts). The markers indicate the raglan lines. The pattern "breaks" at raglan lines. Work in pattern following chart. To center the pattern on front and back, begin with 10th (3rd, 16th, 11th, 4th, 17th) st of chart. To center pattern on the sleeves, begin with 17th (16th, 15th, 14th, 13th, 7th) st. The pattern will "break" at the purl st and raglan lines. Knit 4 (8, 8, 8, 10, 12) rnds without decreasing.

Raglan Shaping: Knit until 2 sts before purl st. K2tog, p1, k1, sl 1, k1, psso (or ssk).
You will decrease at different rates on the body and sleeves. On the sleeves, decrease on every 4th rnd 4

times, on every other rnd 8 times, and then on every rnd 19 (21, 23, 25, 27, 30) times. *At the same time*, on the front and back, decrease on every other rnd 16 times and on every rnd 19 (21, 23, 25, 27, 30) times. After all decreases, 128 (148, 160, 164, 196, 236) sts rem. Now work back and forth, continuing raglan decreases as est. At center front, BO or place on holder the center 23 (25, 29, 31, 33, 35) sts. Continue in pattern following chart. *At the same time*, BO or place 8,6,4,2 (8,6,4,2,2; 8,6,4,2,2,2; 8,6,4,4,2,2,2; 8,6,4,4,2,2,2,2; 8,6,4,4,2,2,2,2,2) sts on a holder on each side of front neck. The total st count for neckband = 112 (120, 120, 128, 132, 132) sts. Change to smaller circular (or use a needle in a larger size for a looser neckband) and Pine Needles only. Work 20 rnds k1, p1 ribbing. BO loosely in ribbing.

FINISHING

Seam underarms. Fold neck band in half and sew down smoothly on WS. Weave in all ends neatly on WS. Gently steam press pullover under damp pressing cloth.

⚹ MAREN'S SHIRT

SKILL LEVEL
Experienced

SIZES
XS/S (M/L, XL/XXL)

FINISHED MEASUREMENTS
Chest: approx. 39½ (47¼, 55¼) in / 100 (120, 140) cm
Total Length: approx. 23¾ (24½, 25¼) in / 60 (62, 64) cm
Sleeve Length: approx. 19¾ (19¾, 19¾) in / 50 (50, 50) cm

YARN
CYCA #1 (fingering) Dale Garn Lille Lerke (53% Merino wool, 47% Egyptian cotton, 155 yd/142 m / 50 g)

YARN COLORS AND AMOUNTS
Half-bleached White 0017: 550 (650, 750) g
Dusty Rose 8121: 100 (100, 150) g
Pink 4425: 50 (50, 50) g
Light Denim 8133: 50 (50, 50) g
Dark Denim Blue 8105: 50 (50, 50) g
Dark Heather 8130: 50 (50, 50) g
Heather 8131: 50 (50, 50) g

SUGGESTED NEEDLE SIZES
U. S. sizes 0 and 1.5 / 2 and 2.5 mm: circulars and sets of 5 dpn.

Note: If you knit stranded colorwork more firmly than single-color knitting, you should go up a needle size.

NOTIONS
2 pairs clasps

GAUGE
28 sts in stockinette or pattern on larger needles = 4 in / 10 cm.
Adjust needle sizes to obtain correct gauge if necessary.

BODY
With White and smaller circular, CO 260 (316, 372) sts. Join, being careful not to twist cast-on row; pm for beginning of rnd. Knit around in stockinette for 1¼ in / 3 cm = facing. Work an eyelet rnd for foldline: *K2tog, yo*; rep * to * around. Pm on this rnd—all subsequent measurements are taken from this point.

Change to larger circular and work in pattern following Chart **A**. Begin at the arrow for your size. After increasing on Row 12 of chart, there are 280 (336, 392) sts. Pm around 1st and 141st (169th, 197th) sts with 139 (167, 195) sts between markers for front and back. After completing Chart **A**, continue in stockinette with White.

When body measures approx. 12¾ (13, 13½) in / 32 (33, 34) cm, decrease the 1 marked st at each side and begin working each side separately.

BACK
= 139 (167, 195) sts. Work back and forth in stockinette with 1 edge st at each side. Always knit edge sts and do not include in pattern. When body measures 17 (17¼, 17¾) in / 43 (44, 45) cm, work in pattern following Chart **B**. Begin at the arrow for your size. When armhole depth is 10¼ (10¾, 11) in / 26 (27, 28) cm and back measures a total of 22¾ (23¾, 24½) in / 58 (60, 62) cm, BO the center 45 (45, 45) sts for neck.
Work each side separately.

At neck edge, on every other row, BO 2,1 sts = 44 (58, 72) sts rem for shoulder.
BO rem sts when armhole depth is 11 (11½, 11¾) in / 28 (29, 30) cm and back measures 23¾ (24½, 25¼) in / 60 (62, 64) cm. Work opposite side to correspond.

FRONT
= 139 (167, 195) sts. Work back and forth as for back.

CHART A

repeat

Increase 20 sts evenly

M/L XL/XXL XS/S

CHART B

repeat

Repeat to finished measurements

1st row = RS

XL/XXL XS/S M/L

CHART C

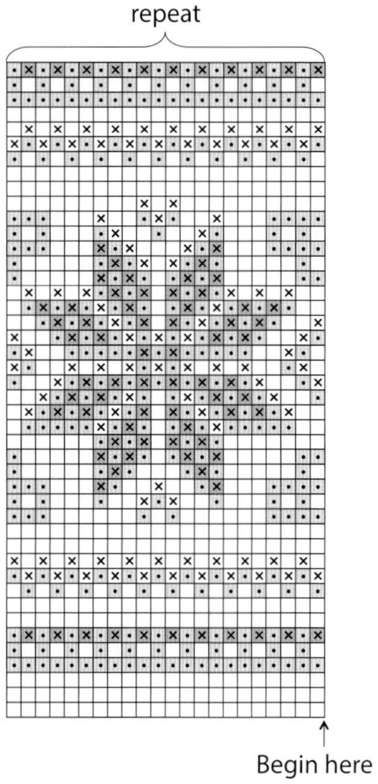

repeat

Begin here

CHART D

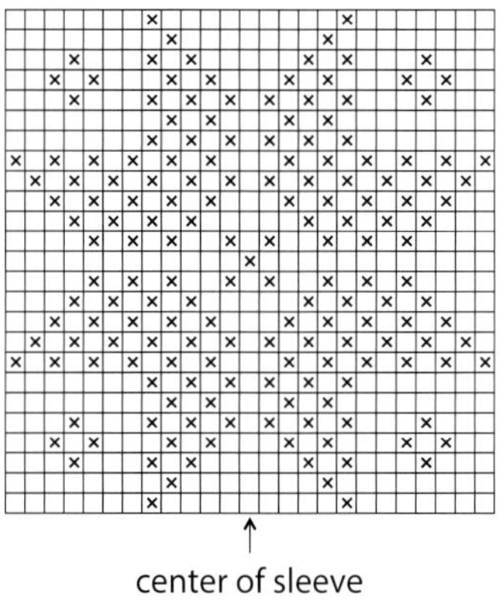

center of sleeve

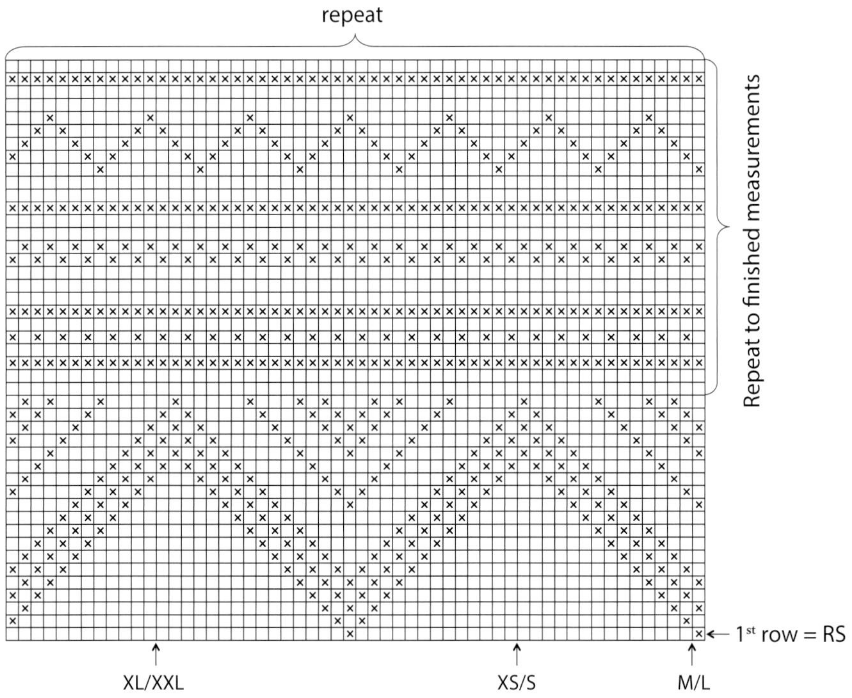

CHART E

repeat

Begin here on
right center section

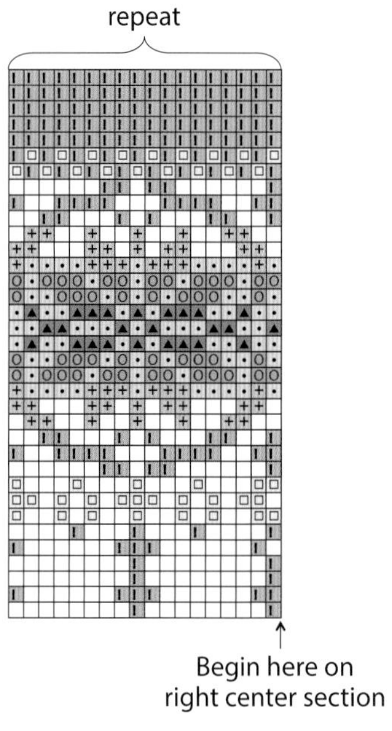

CHART F   **CHART G**

repeat

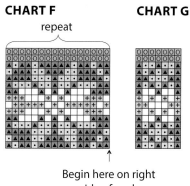

Begin here on right
side of neck

☐   Half-bleached White 0017: knit on RS, purl on WS

☒   Half-bleached White 0017: purl on RS, knit on WS

⊡   Dusty Rose 8121: knit on RS, purl on WS

☒   Dusty Rose 8121: purl on RS, knit on WS

▣   Light Denim 8133

▮   Dark Denim Blue 8105

⊞   Dark Denim Blue 8105

▲   Dark Heather 8130

◉   Pink 4425

⊞   Heather 8131

When armhole depth is ¾ in / 2 cm, place center front 51 (51, 51) sts on a holder for neck = 44 (58, 72) sts on each side. Work each side separately. On the next row, CO 1 edge st at neck and continue in stockinette with 1 edge st at each side. When armhole and total length are same as for back, BO rem sts.

SLEEVES

With White and smaller dpn, CO 66 (66, 66) sts. Divide sts onto dpn and join; pm on 1st st = center of underarm. Knit around in stockinette for 1¼ in / 3 cm = facing. On next rnd, work an eyelet rnd for foldline: *K2tog, yo*; rep * to * around. Pm on this rnd—all subsequent measurements are taken from this point.

Change to larger dpn and work in pattern following Chart **C**. After completing Chart **C**, work in stockinette with White. When sleeve measures 5½ in / 14 cm, work next rnd as follows: K1 (marked st at center of underarm), *M1 (lift strand between 2 sts and knit into back loop), k2;*; rep * to * 16 (13, 10) times. (M1, k1) 1 (13, 25) times; (M1, k2) 16 (13, 10) times, M1 = 100 (106, 112) sts.

Continue in stockinette. When piece measures 6 in / 15 cm, M1 at each side of marked sts. Increase every ¾ in / 2 cm 9 more times = 120 (126, 132) sts. When piece measures 13¾ in / 35 cm, work in pattern following Chart **D** centered up sleeve. *At the same time*, increase for gusset below underarm: M1 on each side of marked st = 3 sts for gusset. Continue

increasing the same way, on each side of gusset on every other rnd, 26 more times, with 2 more sts between increases each time = 54 sts increased and 55 sts in gusset.

After completing Chart **D**, continue in stockinette. When 6 increases rem to be worked in gusset, work 31 sts centered on sleeve as follows: *Sl 2 knitwise at the same time, k1, psso (= centered double decrease), p1*; rep * to * 8 times omitting p1 on last rep = 16 sts decreased over the 31 sts. Continue in stockinette, increasing for gusset as est, but, on the 15 sts centered on sleeve, work as follows: *k1tbl, p1*; rep * to * 7 times, ending with p1. After all increases for the gusset, there are 158 (164, 170) sts and sleeve is approx. 19¾ in/ 50 cm long.

BO all sts around. Make the second sleeve the same way.

CENTER FRONT

Slip center front sts on holder to larger circular. With White and WS facing out, CO 1 edge st at each side and work back and forth in stockinette for ¾ in / 2 cm (= facing). BO.

Pick up and knit sts along front neck, inside edge sts, as follows: 14 sts per 2 in / 5 cm down along right side, CO 5 extra steek sts, pick up and knit 14 sts per 2 in / 5 cm down left side (= same number of sts as along right side), CO 5 extra steek sts (= outer steek). Do not pick up sts along back neck or along lower opening.

Work around in pattern following Chart **E** but do not work steek sts in pattern. Make sure pattern begins and ends the same way at top and bottom on right and left front edges. When pattern is complete, pm (= foldline). Work another 6 rnds with Dark Denim Blue (= facing). BO.

Reinforce each steek by machine-stitching 2 lines on each side of center steek st. Carefully cut each steek open up center st. Turn facing to WS and sew down smoothly.

Seam right and left fronts about 1¼ in / 3 cm from lower edge, making sure stitches are not visible. Stitch center piece to body at lower edge, inside steek sts. Securely sew facing on WS to cover cut edges. Use duplicate st to embroider the bottom 9 rows of Chart E below center front piece, making sure that pattern is centered (see photos).

FINISHING
Sew or Kitchener st to join shoulders. Baste rounded neck opening, which is as wide as the whole center piece, about 2 (2½, 2½) in / 5 (6, 6) cm deep. Machine-stitch above basting line. Cut away extra fabric.

NECKBAND
With larger circular and Pink, pick up and knit about 14 sts per 2 in / 5 cm around neck. You'll need an odd number of sts. Pm around 7 sts at center back. Work back and forth, beginning on WS with a purl row. On next row, knit 1 edge st at each side and work pattern following Chart **F** between edge sts except for the 7 marked sts at center back. Work the 7 center sts following Chart **G**. Make sure that Chart **F** begins and ends the same way at center front and on each side.

After completing pattern, pm for foldline. Change to smaller circular and work stockinette facing: 3 rows Pink and then continue with Heather for the facing until facing (as measured from foldline) is as wide as neckband. BO. Fold neck facing to WS to cover cut steek edges and sew down. Seam openings at both short ends of neckband.

Attach sleeves. Sew on clasps. Weave in all ends neatly on WS.

❧✛SOLVEIG'S TUNIC

SKILL LEVEL
Experienced

SIZES
S (M, L, XL, XXL)

FINISHED MEASUREMENTS
Chest: approx. 40½ (43, 45¾, 48, 50¾) in / 103 (109, 116, 122, 129) cm
Total Length: approx. 26¾ (27½, 28, 28¼) in / 66 (68, 70, 71, 72) cm
Sleeve Length: approx. 22½ (22½, 22½, 22½, 22½) in / 57 (57, 57, 57, 57) cm

YARN
CYCA #1 (fingering) Viking of Norway Alpaca Fine (85% superfine alpaca, 15% Highland wool, 182 yd/166 m / 50 g)
CYCA #1 (fingering) Viking of Norway Baby Ull (100% superwash Merino wool, 190 yd/175 m / 50 g)

YARN COLORS AND AMOUNTS
BABY ULL
Pearl Gray 312: 300 (300, 350, 400, 400) g
Light Gray 313: 100 (100, 100, 150, 150) g
Denim Blue 325: 100 (100, 100, 100, 100) g

ALPACA FINE
White 600: 50 (50, 50, 50, 100) g
Light Pink 665: 50 (50, 50, 50, 50) g
Dark Pink 660: 50 (50, 50, 50, 50) g
Heather 670: 50 (50, 50, 50, 50) g
Royal Blue 622: 50 (50, 50, 50, 50) g
Light Blue 624: 50 (50, 50, 50, 50) g
Navy Blue 625: 100 (100, 100, 100, 150) g

SUGGESTED NEEDLE SIZES
U. S. sizes 1.5 and 2.5 / 2.5 and 3 mm: circulars and sets of 5 dpn.

Note: If you knit stranded colorwork more firmly than single-color knitting, you should go up a needle size.

NOTIONS
2 pairs clasps
Optional: ribbon for facings

GAUGE
28 sts in stockinette on larger needles = 4 in / 10 cm. Adjust needle sizes to obtain correct gauge if necessary.

BODY
With Alpaca Fine Navy Blue and smaller circular, CO 288 (306, 324, 342, 360) sts. Join, being careful not to twist cast-on row; pm for beginning of rnd. Work around in k1, p1 ribbing for ¾ in / 2 cm. Pm at each side with 143 (153, 161, 171, 179) sts for front and 145 (153, 163, 171, 181) sts for back. Change to larger circular. Work following Chart **A**, beginning at arrow for your size.

When body measures approx. 15½ (15¾, 16¼, 16½, 17) in / 39 (40, 41, 42, 43) cm, place center 59 sts on a holder; CO 5 sts over gap for a steek. The steek sts are not worked in pattern or counted in st counts; 42 (47, 51, 56, 60) sts rem for each front. When body measures approx. 18½ (19, 19¼, 19¼, 19¼) in / 47 (48, 49, 49, 49) cm, BO 18 (21, 25, 28, 32) sts at each side of back and 17 (21, 24, 28, 31) sts at side of both fronts = 35 (42, 49, 56, 63) sts bound off at each side.

On each front 25 (26, 27, 28, 29) sts rem and 109 (111, 113, 115, 117) sts rem on back. On next rnd, CO 5 new sts over bound-of sts at each side. Continue in pattern as before until body measures 26 (26¾, 27½, 28, 28¼) in / 66 (68, 70, 71, 72) cm. BO rem sts.

SLEEVES
With Alpaca Fine Navy Blue and smaller dpn, CO 94 (100, 104, 110, 114) sts. Divide sts onto dpn and join; pm for beginning of rnd. Work around in k1, p1 ribbing for ¾ in / 2 cm. Increase 1 st on last rnd = 95 (101, 105, 111, 115) sts. Now work in pattern following Chart **B**. Count out from center of sleeve to

CHART A

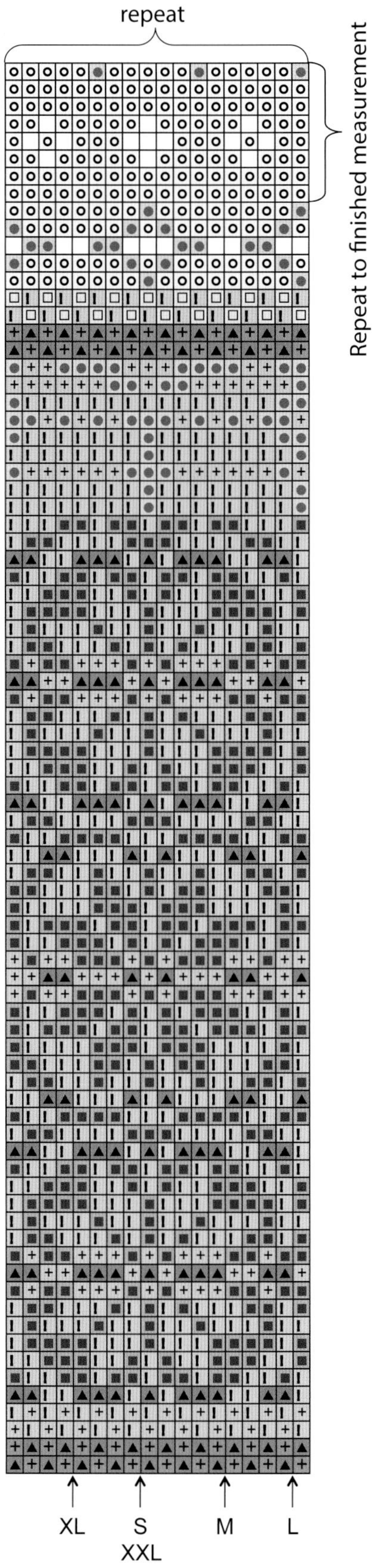

repeat

Repeat to finished measurement

XL S M L
XXL

CHART B

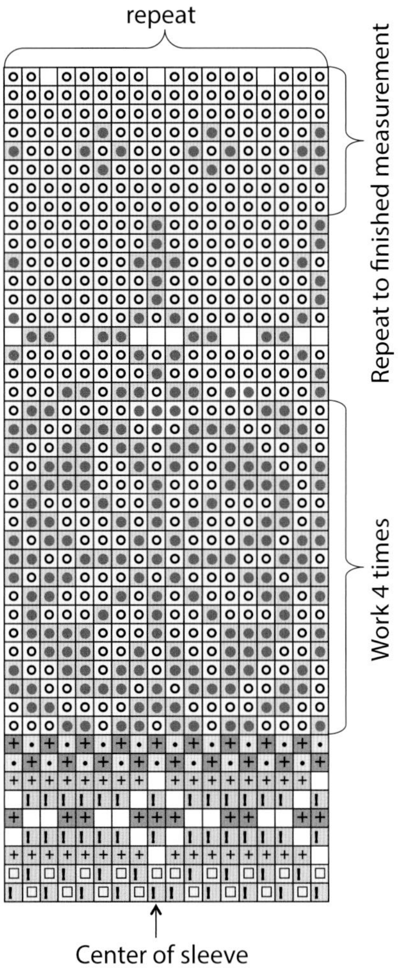

repeat

Repeat to finished measurement

Work 4 times

Center of sleeve

CHART C

repeat

CHART D

repeat

End here
left front

Begin here
right front

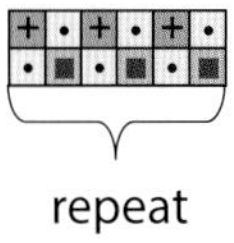

	White 600	ALPACA FINE
	Pearl Grey 312	BABY ULL
	Light Gray 313	BABY ULL
	Light Pink 665	ALPACA FINE
	Dark Pink 660	ALPACA FINE
	Heather 670	ALPACA FINE
	Light Blue 624	ALPACA FINE
	Royal Blue 622	ALPACA FINE
	Denim Blue 325	BABY ULL
	Navy Blue 625	ALPACA FINE

determine where to begin pattern. Make sure pattern is centered on sleeve.

When sleeve is 17 (16¼, 16, 15½, 15) in / 43 (41.5, 40.5, 39, 38) cm long, divide at center of sleeve and begin working back and forth for 2½ (3, 3¼, 4, 4¼) in / 6 (7.5, 8.5, 10, 11) cm. Sleeve should now measure 19¼ in / 49 cm.

For sleeve cap, at each side, on every other row, place 2 sts on holder 7 (7, 6, 6, 5) times and 3 sts 7 (7, 8, 8, 9) times. Transfer all sts back to needle and, with WS facing, work back and forth in stockinette for ¾ in / 2 cm for facing. BO.

Make the second sleeve the same way.

FINISHING
Reinforce each steek by machine-stitching 2 lines on each side of center steek st. Carefully cut each steek open up center st.

CENTER FRONT PIECE
Place held center front sts onto larger size needle. Cast on 1 edge st (knit edge sts on all rows) at each side and work back and forth in pattern following Chart **C**. After completing charted pattern, BO with Dark Pink. Sew on at each side inside steek and edge sts.

With Pearl Gray and larger circular, pick up and knit sts along front neck, inside steek sts: pick up and knit 14 sts per 2 in / 5 cm along right side, CO 5 extra sts for steek, pick up and knit 14 sts per 2 in / 5 cm along left side (= same number of sts as for right side), CO 5 extra sts for steek. Do not pick up sts along back of neck or along lower opening. Work around in pattern following Chart **D**, but do not work steek sts in pattern. Make sure pattern begins and ends the same way at top and bottom of right and left front pieces. *At the same time*, decrease 1 st on each side at top of steek for neck: On every rnd 11 times, on every other rnd 5 times, and, on every 4th rnd 1 time. Decrease *before* the steek with ssk and *after* steek with k2tog. When pattern is complete, pm for foldline. Work another 1¼ in / 3 cm in stockinette with Navy Blue for facing, BO.

Reinforce each steek by machine-stitching 2 lines on each side of center steek st at neck and below in Pattern **C**. Carefully cut steek open up center st.

Turn facing to WS and sew down smoothly. Sew together, as invisibly as possible, about 4 in / 10 cm at lower edge of right and left fronts. Stitch Pattern **C** to lower fronts inside steek sts. Sew or Kitchener st to join shoulders.

NECKBAND
With Navy Blue and larger circular, pick up and knit sts about 14 sts per 2 in / 5 cm along neck, inside steek sts. Work 12 rows back and forth in stockinette. BO. Fold neckband to WS and sew down securely to cover cut edges.

Attach sleeves so that split at top matches side seams. Fold facings to WS and sew down to cover cut edges. If desired, hand stitch ribbon on WS to cover cut edges of neckband. Weave in all ends neatly on WS. Sew on clasps.

KNUT'S PULLOVER

SKILL LEVEL
Experienced

SIZES
S (M, L, XL, XXL)

FINISHED MEASUREMENTS
Chest: approx. 38½ (43, 47¼, 51½, 56) in / 98 (109, 120, 131, 142) cm
Total Length: approx. 26¾ (27½, 28¼, 29¼, 30) in / 68 (70, 72, 74, 76) cm
Sleeve Length: approx. 19¾ (19¾, 19¾, 19¾, 19¾) in / 50 (50, 50, 50, 50) cm

YARN
CYCA #3 (DK, light worsted) Du Store Alpakka Sterk (40% finest alpaca, 40% Merino wool, 20% nylon, 150 yd/137 m / 50 g)
CYCA #3 (DK, light worsted) Dale Garn Falk (100% South American wool, 116 yd/106 m / 50 g)

YARN COLORS AND AMOUNTS
STERK
Gray-Black Mouliné 808: 350 (400, 450, 450, 500) g
White 851: 50 (50, 50, 50, 50) g
Cornflower 840: 50 (50, 50, 50, 50) g
Denim 865: 50 (50, 50, 50, 50) g
Dark Pink 825: 50 (50, 50, 50, 50) g
Red 828: 50 (50, 50, 50, 50) g
Linden Green 847: 50 (50, 50, 50, 50) g

FALK
Gray Heather 0007: 300 (300, 350, 350, 400) g
Light Gray 6031: 50 (50, 50, 50, 50) g
Dark Olive 9905: 50 (50, 50, 50, 50) g

SUGGESTED NEEDLE SIZES
U. S. sizes 4 and 6 / 3.5 and 4 mm: circulars and sets of 5 dpn.

Note: If you knit stranded colorwork more firmly than single-color knitting, you should go up a needle size.

NOTIONS
1 button
Optional: ribbon for facings

GAUGE
22 sts in stockinette on larger needles = 4 in / 10 cm. Adjust needle sizes to obtain correct gauge if necessary.

BODY
With Sterk Gray-Black Mouliné and smaller circular, CO 252 (280, 308, 336, 364) sts. Join, being careful not to twist cast-on row; pm for beginning of rnd. Work around in k3, p4 ribbing for 2¾ in / 7 cm. On the last rnd, decrease all the purl ribs from 4 to 3 sts = 216 (240, 264, 288, 312) sts rem. Pm at each side with 107 (119, 131, 143, 155) sts for front and 109 (121, 133, 145, 157) sts for back. Change to larger circular. Knit 1 rnd and then work following Chart **A**, beginning at arrow for your size.

After completing Chart **A**, work Chart **B**, beginning at arrow for your size for both front and back (the pattern will be offset at both side seams for sizes M, L, and XL).

When body measures approx. 19¼ (19¾, 20, 20½, 21) in / 49 (50, 51, 52, 53) cm, BO 8 (10, 12, 14, 16) sts centered at each side for armholes = 4 (5, 6, 7, 8) sts on each side of side marker. On front, 99 (109, 119, 129, 139) sts rem and 101 (111, 121, 131, 141) sts rem on back. Measure down 16¼ in / 41 cm from bind-off row and pm. This will be the reference point for beginning the pattern on sleeves.

SLEEVES
With Falk Dark Olive and smaller dpn, CO 60 (60, 66, 66, 72) sts. Divide sts onto dpn and join. Work 8 rnds in stockinette for facing, increase 5 sts evenly spaced around on last rnd = 65 (65, 71, 71, 77) sts. Pm = foldline; all subsequent measurements are taken from this point. Work following Chart **C**, making

CHART A

repeat

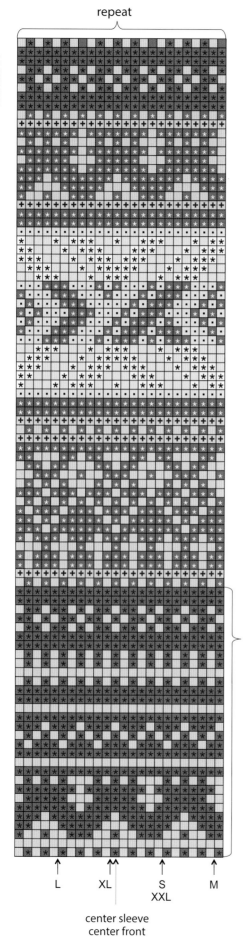

L   XL   S   M
     XXL

center sleeve
center front

	Gray Heather 0007	FALK
⊞	On body: Grey Heather 0007	FALK
	On sleeves: Denim 865	STERK
·	On body: Gray-Black Mouliné 808S	TERK
	On sleeves: Light Gray 6031	FALK
	On body: Gray-Black Mouliné 808	STERK
	On sleeves: White 851	STERK
✶	On body: Gray-Black Mouliné 808	STERK
	On sleeves: Cornflower 840	STERK
✭	On body: Grey Heather 0007	FALK
	On sleeves: Denim 865	STERK
✦	Gray-Black Mouliné 808	STERK
+	Red 828	STERK
·	Dark Pink 825	STERK
		Linden Green 847	STERK
⊞	Dark Olive 9905	FALK
◉	Cornflower 840	STERK

CHART C

repeat

Center sleeve
Center front

On body, work repeat until piece measures approx. 7 (7½, 8, 8¼, 8¾) in / 18 (19, 20, 21, 22) cm—the size and gauge will affect how the repeat will work out.

Make sure to end after a single-color row on the chart.

Continue after bracketed section.

On the sleeve, begin at marked reference point and work repeat until sleeve measures approx. 7½ in / 19 cm. End on same chart row as on body.

Continue after bracketed section.

92

CHART B

repeat

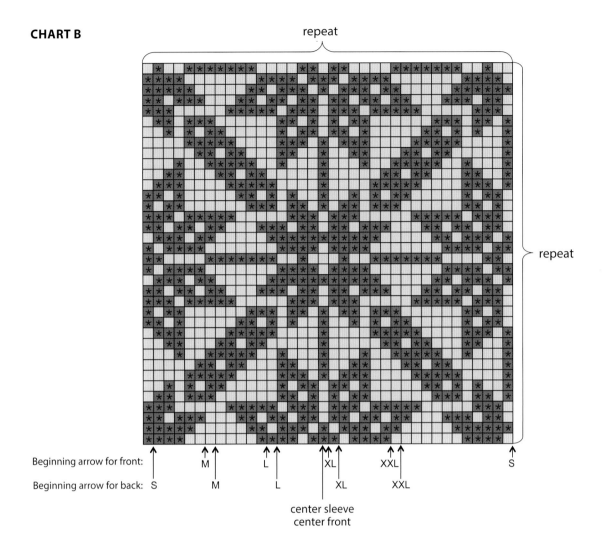

repeat

Beginning arrow for front:

M   L   XL   XXL   S

Beginning arrow for back: S   M   L   XL   XXL

center sleeve
center front

sure pattern is centered on sleeve. Change to Sterk Gray-Black Mouliné. Knit 1 rnd, increasing in 1st st = 66 (66, 72, 72, 78) sts. Work 1 rnd, k3, p3 ribbing. On next rnd, increase purl ribs from 3 to 4 sts each = 77 (77, 84, 84, 91) sts. Work around in k3, p4 ribbing until sleeve measures 3½ in / 9 cm above foldline.

On the last rnd, decrease all purl ribs from 4 to 3 sts = 66 (66, 72, 72, 78) sts rem. Change to larger dpn. Knit 1 rnd, and, at the same time, increase evenly spaced around to 67 (69, 73, 75, 79) sts. Now work following Chart **A** and then Chart **B**. Count out from center of sleeve to determine where to begin pattern. Make sure pattern is centered on sleeve. Also, on Chart **A**, use your reference point marker on the body to know which row to start on.

At the same time, when sleeve is 4 in / 10 cm long

(from marker), increase 2 sts centered on underarm. Increase the same way every 3¼ (2¾, 2¾, 2½, 2½) in / 8 (7, 7, 6, 6) cm another 4 (5, 5, 6, 6) times = 77 (81, 85, 89, 93) sts. Work new sts into pattern. When sleeve is 19¾ in / 50 cm long, BO 8 (10, 12, 14, 16) sts centered on underarm = 69 (71, 73, 75, 77) sts rem. Make sure that the underarm bind-off is on same pattern row as on body.

Set sleeve aside while you knit second sleeve the same way.

YOKE
Note: Read through this entire section before you begin knitting.

Place body and sleeves on larger circular = 338 (362, 386, 410, 434) sts total. Pm in first and last sts on front and back. Always work marked sts as p1 with Sterk Gray-Black Mouliné. Otherwise, continue in pattern following chart B on sleeves, front, and back. At the same time, decrease on both armholes and sleeve cap as follows: Decrease 1 st at each side of front and back, on every rnd 4 (7, 10, 13, 16) times; on every other rnd 2 times; and on every 4th rnd 1 time—but omit this last decrease on the front, so the pattern will match when you get to the shoulders.

Now 87 (91, 95, 99, 103) sts rem on back and 21 (22, 23, 24, 25) sts on each front (after sts are set aside for neck—see below). *When decreasing before marked st:* K2tog tbl before marked st in color as for pattern. When decreasing after marked st: K2tog in color as for pattern.

At the same time, decrease 1 st on each side of both sleeves as follows:
On every rnd, 2 (1, 0, 0, 0) times, on every other rnd, 15 (16, 17, 17, 17) times, and on every rnd 2 (1, 0, 0, 0) times.

When armhole depth is 1¼ in / 3 cm, place the center front 45 (47, 49, 51, 53) sts on a holder for neck. On next rnd, CO 4 new sts over the gap for steek (do not work steek sts in pattern or include in st counts). Continue in pattern, decreasing as est. After completing sleeve shaping, place the rem 31 (35, 39, 41, 43) sts of each sleeve on a holder. The body should now measure approx. 24 (24½, 24¾, 25¼, 25½) 61 (62, 63, 64, 65) cm and the sleeves approx. 24½ in / 62 cm total. Now work front and back separately.

BACK

= 87 (91, 95, 99, 103) sts. CO 1 edge st at each side = 89 (93, 97, 101, 105) sts. Work back and forth following Chart **B** as est, beginning and ending each row with k2 with Sterk Gray-Black Mouliné (= edge st + 1 st). Continue as est for 2¾ (3¼, 3½, 4, 4¼) in / 7 (8, 9, 10, 11) cm. Piece should measure approx. 26¾ (27½, 28¼, 29¼, 30) in / 68 (70, 72, 74, 76) cm. BO.

The outermost 21 (22, 23, 24, 25) sts + 1 edge st at each side = shoulder sts.

FRONT

= 21 (22, 23, 24, 25) sts for each half of front + 4 steek sts. Work as for back.

SLEEVES

= 31 (35, 39, 41, 43) sts. Work back and forth in pattern as est, and, on each side of sleeve cap, on every row, BO 2,3 sts. BO rem sts on next row.

FINISHING

Reinforce center front steek by machine-stitching 2 lines on each side of center steek st. Carefully cut steek open up center st. Sew or Kitchener st to join shoulders.

NECKBAND

With Sterk Gray-Black Mouliné and smaller circular, and beginning at left shoulder seam, pick up and knit approx. 11 sts per 2 in / 5 cm down to the 45 (47, 49, 51, 53) sts held for neck, knit held sts and pick up and knit sts up rest of neck. Make sure you have the same number of sts on right and left sides of front and that total st count is a multiple of 6.

Pm on each side of the 45 (47, 49, 51, 53) center front sts. Work around in Pattern **C**, counting out from the center to determine beginning of pattern so it is centered on neck. *At the same time*, decrease 1 st on each side of both markers on every other rnd (= on the 2nd, 4th, and 6th rnds).

Change to Sterk Gray-Black Mouliné, knit 1 rnd and, *at the same time*, BO the center front 39 (41, 43, 45, 47) sts = all the sts between markers. Move beginning of rnd marker to before the bound-off sts and continue back and forth as follows:
Row 1 (WS): K1 edge st (always knit edge sts), purl to last st, end k1 edge st. *At the same time*, adjust st count to be a multiple of 3 - 1.
Row 2 (RS): Work in k2, p1 ribbing with 1 edge st on each side. Begin and end with k2 in ribbing.
Row 3: Work as est, increasing all the k1 to k2 (as sts face you) in ribbing.

Continue in ribbing with 1 edge st on each side until collar measures approx. 2¾ in / 7 cm. On next row, WS, increase every p2 to p3 along back neck (=

over back) but not along both sides of front neck. Continue in ribbing with 1 edge st at each side, until ribbing measures 5½ (5½, 6, 6, 6¼) in / 14 (14, 15, 15, 16) cm.

BO loosely on WS with knit over knit and purl over purl. If the bind-off seems too tight, try this looser method: BO as usual but, at the same time, increase 1 st with M1p between the 2 purl sts. Bind off new purl st as for other sts. Sew left side of collar down at bound-off sts and sew right side of collar behind it (see photo, page 90).

FINISHING
Seam underarms and attach sleeve caps. Sew or crochet a button loop with Sterk Gray-Black Mouliné on bound-off edge of collar, 1½ in / 4 cm up from lower edge. Sew on button opposite loop. Weave in all ends neatly on WS.

BENEDIKTE'S CARDIGAN

SKILL LEVEL
Experienced

SIZES
S (M, L, XL, XXL)

FINISHED MEASUREMENTS
Chest: approx. 34¼ (37¾, 41¼, 45¼, 48¾) in / 87 (96, 105, 115, 124) cm

Circumference: below chest, approx. 32 (35½, 39, 41¼, 42½, 46½) in / 81 (90, 99, 108, 118) cm; at lower edge, approx. 44 (47¾, 51¼, 54¾, 58¼) in / 112 (121, 130, 139, 148) cm

Total Length: approx. 31 (32, 32¾, 33½, 34¼) in / 79 (81, 83, 85, 87) cm

Sleeve Length: to armhole, approx. 17 (17, 17¼, 17¼, 17¾) in / 43 (43, 44, 44, 45) cm

YARN
CYCA #6 (super bulky) Du Store Alpakka Pus (70% baby alpaca, 17% acrylic, 13% polyamide, 109 yd/100 m / 50 g)

CYCA #1 (fingering) Du Store Alpakka Alpakka Wool (60% finest alpaca, 40% pure new wool, 182 yd/ 166 m / 50 g)

YARN COLORS AND AMOUNTS
PUS
Light Gray 4011: 350 (400, 450, 450, 500) g

ALPAKKA WOOL
White 533: 50 (50, 50, 50, 50) g
Dark Green Heather 503: 50 (50, 50, 50, 50) g
Brown Heather 506: 50 (50, 50, 50, 50) g
Dusty Dove Blue 509: 50 (50, 50, 50, 50) g
Dark Turquoise 515: 50 (50, 50, 50, 50) g
Light Apple Green 531: 50 (50, 50, 50, 50) g
Dark Lilac 514: 50 (50, 50, 50, 50) g
Light Denim 529: 50 (50, 50, 50, 50) g
Cerise 512: 50 (50, 50, 50, 50) g

SUGGESTED NEEDLE SIZES
U. S. sizes 2.5 and 11 / 3 and 8 mm: circulars and sets of 5 dpn.

Note: If you knit stranded colorwork more firmly than single-color knitting, you should go up a needle size.

NOTIONS
2 sets clasps
Optional: 3¼ in / 80 mm wide elastic or fusible vlieseline (for waistband)

GAUGE
13 sts in stockinette with Pus on larger needles = 4 in / 10 cm.
27 sts in stockinette with Alpakka Wool on smaller needles = 4 in / 10 cm.
Adjust needle sizes to obtain correct gauge if necessary.

STITCHES AND TECHNIQUES

SEED STITCH
Row/Rnd 1: *K1, p1*; rep * to *.
Row/Rnd 2: Work purl over knit and knit over purl. Rep Rows/Rnds 1-2.

DECREASING IN LACE PATTERNS
Work carefully when decreasing in lace patterns. If the decreases come within the lace yarnover and decrease pairings, work those stitches in stockinette or seed stitch instead (whichever works into the surrounding pattern).

INCREASING IN LACE PATTERNS
Work carefully when increasing in lace patterns. If the increases come within the lace yarnover and decrease pairings, work those stitches in stockinette or seed stitch instead (whichever works into the surrounding pattern).

CHART A

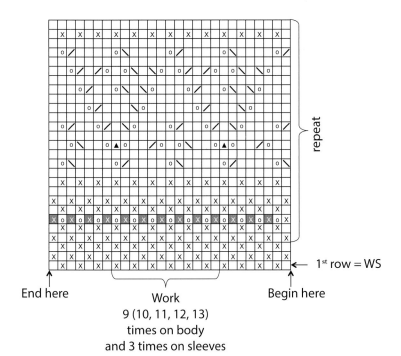

1st row = WS

End here

Begin here

Work
9 (10, 11, 12, 13)
times on body
and 3 times on sleeves

repeat

CHART B

repeat

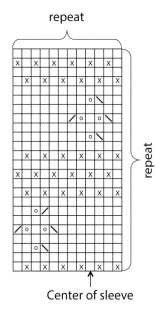

repeat

Center of sleeve

☐		Knit on RS, purl on WS
☒		Purl on RS, knit on WS
◦		Yo
◣		Sl 1, k1, psso or ssk
◿		K2tog
▨		P2tog
▲		Sl 2 knitwise at same time, k1, psso (= centered double decrease)

CHART C

repeat

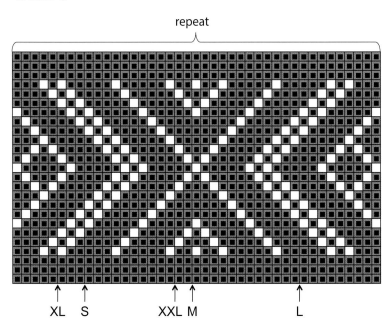

XL   S   XXL M   L

CHART D

repeat

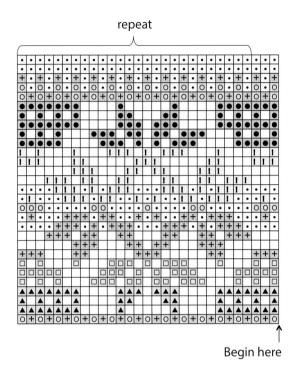

Begin here

CHART E

repeat

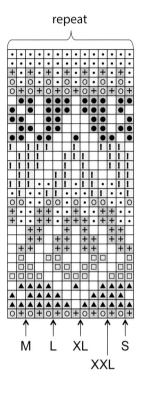

M   L   XL   S

XXL

☐ White 553

■ Dark Gray Heather 503

⦿ Brown Heather 506

· Dusty Dove Blue 509

▲ Dark Turquoise 515

⊡ Light Apple Green 531

⊞ Dark Lilac 514

Ⅰ Light Denim 529

◙ Cerise 512

CARDIGAN

The lower section, yoke, sleeves, waistband, and front bands are each worked separately and then joined in finishing.

LOWER SECTION

With Pus Light Gray and larger circular, CO 145 (157, 169, 181, 193) sts. Pm on each side of the center 73 (79, 85, 91, 97) sts for back; with 36 (39, 42, 45, 48) sts on each side for each front. Work back and forth as follows:

Set-up Row: 11 seed sts (see Stitches and Techniques above), pattern following Chart **A** = 123 (135, 147, 159, 171) sts, 11 seed sts.
Continue as est.

At the same time, when piece measures 4 (4¼, 4¾, 5¼, 5½) in / 10 (11, 12, 13, 14) cm, decrease 1 st at each side of both markers (see Decreasing in Lace Patterns above). Rep the decreases every 1¼ in / 3 cm another 9 times = 105 (117, 129, 141, 153) sts rem, with 53 (59, 65, 71, 77) sts for back and 26 (29, 32, 35, 38) sts for each front. When piece measures

15¾ (16¼, 16½, 17, 17¼) in / 40 (41, 42, 43, 44) cm, BO. Mark the chart where you began and ended the front and back.

YOKE

With Pus Light Gray and larger circular, CO 85 (97, 109, 121, 133) sts. Pm on each side of the center 53 (59, 65, 71, 77) sts for back; with 16 (19, 22, 25, 28) sts on each side for each front + 1 edge st. Work back and forth in pattern following Chart **A** with 1 edge st on each side. Begin on desired row in pattern and begin and end at the markers from lower piece on chart. Knit edge sts on every row.

When piece measures 1½ in / 4 cm, increase 1 st at each side of both side markers. *At the same time*, decrease 1 st for V-neck inside 1 edge st at beginning and end of row. The increased sts should be worked into pattern. Rep this increase/decrease every 1½ in / 4 cm as follows: Increase at sides another 1 time = 57 (63, 69, 75, 81) sts on back. Decrease for front neck another 5 (6, 6, 6, 6) times. *At the same time*, when yoke measures 4¾ in / 12 cm (all sizes), BO 4

(4, 6, 8, 8) sts at each side for armholes. Now work each side separately.

BACK
= 53 (59, 63, 67, 73) sts. Work back and forth in pattern as est. *At the same time*, shape armholes on each side: on every other row, BO 2,1 (2,1,1,1; 2,2,1,1; 2,2,1,1,1; 3,2,2,1,1) sts = 47 (49, 51, 53, 55) sts rem. When armhole depth is 6¼ (6¾, 7, 7½, 8) in / 16 (17, 18, 19, 20) cm, work the center 33 (35, 35, 35, 35) sts in seed st. When armhole depth is 7½ (8, 8¼, 8¾, 9) in / 19 (20, 21, 22, 23) cm and piece measures a total of 12¼ (12¾, 13, 13½, 13¾) in / 31 (32, 33, 34, 35) cm, BO 18 (18, 19, 20, 20) sts at each side for shoulders.

FRONT
Work back and forth in pattern and shape armholes on each side: on every other row, BO 1,1 (2,1,1; 2,1,1,1; 2,2,1,1; 3,2,1,1,1) sts. *At the same time*, continue shaping neck. After all decreases, 8 (8, 9, 10, 11) sts remain for shoulder. When front is same length as back, BO as for back.

SLEEVES
With Pus Light Gray and larger dpn, CO 51 sts (all sizes). Divide sts onto dpn. Work around in pattern following Chart **A**, 1 time in length. On the last rnd, adjust st count to 43 (45, 47, 49, 53) sts. Continue in pattern following Chart **B** for rest of sleeve. Count out from the center st to determine where to begin pattern. When sleeve is 17 (17, 17¼, 17¼, 17¾) in / 43 (43, 44, 44, 45) cm long, BO 4 (4, 6, 8, 8) sts centered on underarm = 39 (41, 41, 41, 45) sts rem. Now work back and forth and decrease at each side on every other row: 2 sts 1 time, 1 st until sleeve cap measures approx. 4¾ in / 12 cm, 2 sts 1 time, 3 sts 1 time, BO rem sts. Sleeve cap is now approx. 5½ in / 14 cm long and total sleeve length is approx. 22½ (22½, 22¾, 22¾, 23¼) in / 57 (57, 58, 58, 59) cm. Knit the second sleeve the same way.

WAISTBAND
With Alpakka Wool Dark Gray and smaller circular, CO 215 (239, 263, 289, 315) sts. Work back and forth in stockinette for 12 rows = facing. CO 6 sts for center front steek (steek sts are not worked in pattern). Join and knit around in pattern following Chart **C**, beginning at arrow for your size. After completing Chart **C**, BO steek sts and work back and forth in stockinette = facing. Use another color for facing so you don't run out of Dark Gray. BO when both facings, when held together, are ³/₈ in / 1 cm wider than pattern section.

Reinforce center front steek by machine-stitching 2 lines on each side of center steek st. Carefully cut steek open up center st.

FRONT BANDS
With Alpakka Wool Dusty Dove Blue and smaller circular, CO 176 (182, 188, 194, 200) sts. Join, being careful not to twist cast-on row; pm for beginning of rnd. Knit 2 rnds.
Next Rnd: Work 5 steek sts, pattern following Chart **D** over 83 (86, 89, 92, 95) sts = right front band, 5 steek sts, pattern following Chart **E** over rem 83 (86, 89, 92, 95) sts = left front band. Begin at chart arrow for your size. On last rnd, BO steek sts. Place sts for right and left front bands each on separate holders.

Reinforce each steek by machine-stitching 2 lines on each side of center steek st. Carefully cut steek open up center st.

Left Front Band: Place band sts onto smaller circular. With Alpakka Wool Dusty Dove Blue, knit across. At end of row (as seen from right side), pick up and knit 20 sts along one short side of waistband—pick up inside steek sts and only along Chart **B** pattern, not along facing. Work back and forth in stockinette until facing is as wide as Chart **E** pattern. BO.

Right Front Band: Work as for left front band but pick up and knit sts along the other short end of waistband and at beginning of row (instead of end). If you've run out of Dove Blue, use another color for facing.

FINISHING
Waistband: If desired, iron on vlieseline on back of waistband or add elastic of suitable width. Fold facings to WS and join.
Front Bands: Fold facings to WS and join.

Assembly: Sew or Kitchener st to join shoulders. Sew waistband and front bands to yoke. Sew "skirt" below waistband. Attach sleeves.

Optional: Sew ribbon along WS of back neck to cover cut edges of front bands.
Sew clasps to waistband. Weave in all ends neatly on WS.

↗ LINA MARIE'S DRESS

SKILL LEVEL
Experienced

SIZES
S (M, L, XL, XXL)

FINISHED MEASUREMENTS
Chest: approx. 32 (34¾, 37¾, 42½, 47¾) in / 81 (88, 96, 108, 121) cm
Circumference: below chest, approx. 30 (32¼, 35½, 40¼, 45¾) in / 76 (82, 90, 102, 116) cm; at lower edge: approx. 50¾ (50¾, 50¾, 60¾, 60¾) in / 129 (129, 129, 154, 154) cm
Total Length: approx. 53¼ (54, 54¾, 55½, 56¼) in / 135 (137, 139, 141, 143) cm
Sleeve Length: to armhole, approx. 17 (17, 17, 17, 17) in / 43 (43, 43, 43, 43) cm

YARN
CYCA #1 (fingering) Viking of Norway Baby Ull (100% superwash Merino wool, 190 yd/175 m / 50 g)
CYCA #1 (fingering) Viking of Norway Alpaca Fine (85% superfine alpaca, 15% highland wool, 182 yd/166 m / 50 g)

YARN COLORS AND AMOUNTS
BABY ULL
Blue 323: 350 (400, 450, 500, 550) g
Pearl Gray 312: 100 (100, 150, 150, 150) g
Light Blue 320: 100 (100, 100, 150, 150) g
Denim Blue 325: 100 (100, 100, 150, 150) g

ALPACA FINE
White 600: 250 (300, 300, 350, 400) g
Dark Blue 626: 503: 100 (100, 100, 150, 150) g
Royal Blue 622: 50 (50, 50, 50, 50) g

YARN FOR BELT (amounts for all sizes)
BABY ULL
Light Pink 364: 50 g
Light Blue 320: 50 g
Petroleum 379: 50 g

ALPACA FINE
Light Green 631: 50 g
Pastel Pink 664: 50 g
Coral 648: 50 g
Ochre 618: 50 g
Cognac 653: 50 g

SUGGESTED NEEDLE SIZES
U. S. sizes 1.5 and 2.5 / 2.5 and 3 mm: circulars and sets of 5 dpn.

Note: If you knit stranded colorwork more firmly than single-color knitting, you should go up a needle size.

NOTIONS
Optional: ribbon for facings
2½ in / 6 cm wide elastic long enough to go around below chest + seam allowance.
If you can't find the suggested width of elastic, sew two strips of 1¼ in / 3 cm wide elastic together.
2 pairs clasps

NOTIONS FOR BELT
Optional: fusible vlieseline
2 pairs clasps

GAUGE
28 sts in stockinette on larger needles = 4 in / 10 cm.
Adjust needle sizes to obtain correct gauge if necessary.

SKIRT
With Alpaca Fine Dark Blue and smaller circular, CO 360 (360, 360, 432, 432) sts. Join, being careful not to twist cast-on row; pm for beginning of rnd. 1st st = center back. Knit around in stockinette for 1½ in / 4 cm for facing. Pm on last rnd—take all subsequent measurements from this point. Change to larger circular. Work in pattern following Chart **A**, beginning at arrow for your size. Next, work following Chart **B** until piece measures approx. 39¾ (40¼, 40½, 41, 41¼) in / 101 (102, 103, 104, 105) cm. Pm and take subsequent measurements from this point.

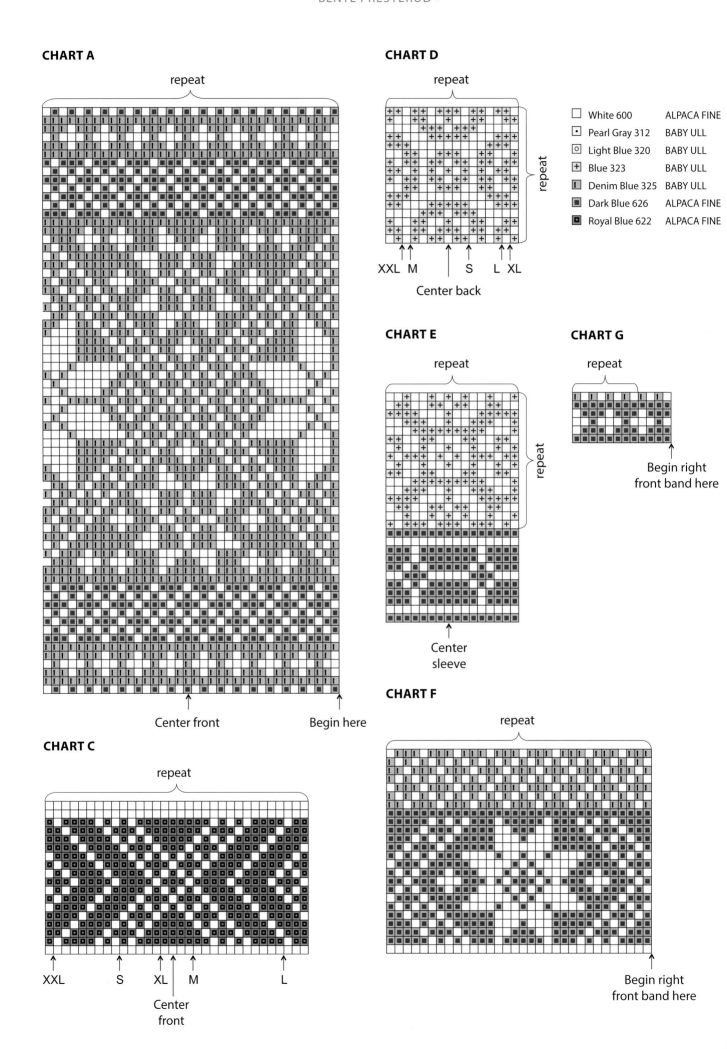

CHART B

repeat

XL
XXL

Center front

S
M
L

WAISTBAND AND YOKE

Change to Alpaca Fine White and knit next rnd as follows:

P1 (center back), k27 (28, 30, 32, 34). Place next 37 (32, 27, 36, 27) sts on a holder (= back pleat), k49 (58, 65, 78, 93). Place next 37 (33, 27, 37, 27) sts on a holder (= front pleat), k55 (57, 61, 65, 69) = center front. Place next 37 (32, 27, 36, 27) sts on a holder (= front pleat), k49 (58, 65, 78, 93). Place next 37 (32, 27, 36, 27) sts on a holder (= back pleat), knit rem 27 (28, 30, 32, 34) sts = 212 (230, 252, 286, 324) sts on needle. Work in pattern following Chart **C**, beginning at arrow for your size. Always work the 1st st of rnd as p1 with MC = center back.

After completing Chart **C**, BO the center front 47 (47, 47, 47, 47) sts for front opening/bands = 165 (183, 205, 239, 277) sts rem. Pm on each side of the center 107 (115, 127, 143, 163) sts (= back), with 29 (34, 39, 48, 57) sts on each side = front pieces. CO 5 new sts over the held sts at center front = steek (do not work steek in pattern or include in st counts). The rnd now begins here. Work in pattern following Chart **D**, beginning at arrow for your size. The 1st st (= center back) is now worked in pattern.

At the same time, increase 1 st at each side of both side markers every ¾ in / 2 cm 4 times = 181 (199, 221, 255, 293) sts with 115 (123, 135, 151, 171) sts for back and 33 38, 43, 52, 61) sts for each front. Work new sts into pattern. When yoke measures 6 in / 15 cm (including waistband), BO 6 (8, 10, 10, 12) sts at each side for armholes = 109 (115, 125, 141, 159) sts for back and 30 (34, 38, 47, 55) sts for each front. Set body side while you knit sleeves.

SLEEVES

With Baby Ull Denim Blue and smaller dpn, CO 53 (57, 59, 63, 65) sts. Divide sts onto dpn and join. Knit 11 rnds in stockinette (= facing). Pm on last rnd—take all subsequent measurements from this point. Change to larger dpn and Alpaca Fine Dark Blue. Knit 1 rnd, increasing 6 sts evenly spaced around = 59 (63, 65, 69, 71) sts. Work around in pattern following Chart **E**. Count out from center of sleeve to determine beginning st for your size. Make sure pattern is centered on sleeve. When sleeve measures

4 in / 10 cm, increase 2 sts centered on underarm. Increase the same way every ¾ in another 12 (12, 14, 16, 19) times = 85 (89, 95, 103, 111) sts. Work new sts into pattern. When sleeve is 17 in / 43 cm long (all sizes), BO 6 (8, 10, 10, 12) sts centered on underarm = 79 (81, 85, 93, 99) sts rem. Set sleeve aside while you knit second sleeve the same way.

YOKE

Place body and sleeve sts on same larger circular with a sleeve at each side of yoke = 327 (345, 371, 421, 467) sts total. Pm at each intersection of body and sleeve. Continue around in pattern as est, but work 1 st at each side of both sleeves as p1 in Baby Ull Blue throughout. That means 1 purl st at each intersection.

At the same time, on 1st rnd, begin shaping V-neck, armholes, and sleeve cap. Decrease 1 st at each side of each purl st st intersections and on each side of center front steek as follows:
Before each purl/steek st, ssk in color fitting in pattern.
After each purl/steek st, k2tog in color fitting in pattern.
Repeat decreases:
On front neck: every ⅜ in / 1 cm a total of 11 (13, 13, 15, 15) times.
On front and back armholes: on every rnd a total of 3 (4, 8, 15, 22) times.
On sleeve caps: on both sleeves on *every* rnd a total of 6 (2, 1, 4, 4) times and then on *every other* rnd 22 (25, 25, 24, 24) times.

After all the decreases, 16 (17, 17, 17, 18) sts rem on each front, 103 (107, 109, 111, 115) sts rem on back, and 23 (27, 33, 37, 43) sts rem on each sleeve cap. Divide yoke at each intersection and work each separately.

SLEEVE CAPS

Work back and forth in pattern and, *at the same time*, at each side on every other row, BO 2,3 sts. BO rem 13 (17, 23, 27, 33) sts.

BACK

CO 1 st at each side for an edge st (knit edge sts on

every row) = 105 (109, 111, 113, 117) sts. Work back and forth in pattern as est, beginning each row with k1 (edge st) + p1 (as seen on RS) and end each row with p1 (as seen on RS) + k1 (edge st). Work the same way for 1½ (2, 2½, 2¾, 3) in / 4 (5, 6, 7, 8) cm. BO 34 (35, 35, 35, 36) sts at each side for shoulders and place rem 37 (39, 41, 43, 45) sts on a holder for back neck.

FRONTS
CO 1 st at each side for an edge st. Work back and forth in pattern as est, but, at outer side of each shoulder, begin each row with k1 (edge st) + p1 (as seen on RS) as on back. Work any remaining neck decreases. BO when same length as back.

FINISHING STEEKS AND FRONT BANDS
Reinforce center front steek by machine-stitching 2 lines on each side of center steek st. Carefully cut steek open up center st.

FRONT BANDS AND NECKBAND
With larger circular and Alpaca Fine White, pick up and knit approx. 14 sts per 2 in / 5 cm along right front edge/neck edge, CO 5 steek sts, and pick up and knit same number of sts along left front and neck edges, CO 5 steek sts. Work around in pattern following Chart **F**, beginning at arrow for right front band. Work in mirror-image down left front to end the same way at bound-off edge. On the last rnd, BO steek sts and place rem sts on a holder.

Reinforce each steek by machine-stitching 2 lines on each side of center steek st. Carefully cut steek open up center st. Join shoulders by sewing or with Kitchener st. Place sts of both front bands and neck back on larger circular and work back and forth in pattern following Chart **G**. *At the same time*, on 1st row, adjust st count along back neck to accommo-date pattern.

Change to smaller needle and Baby Ull Denim Blue. Work back and forth in stockinette for 11 rows for facing. BO. Fold facing to WS and sew down securely.

Join right and left front bands at lower front and up about ¾-1¼ in / 2-3 cm, or more if you want a less

deep opening. Stitch lower edge of front/neckband to waistband's bound-off edge.

FINISHING
Fold in all facings to WS and sew down securely. Join sleeve caps inside 1 edge st. Seam underarms.

Optional: Hand sew ribbon over all cut edges on WS.

Sew elastic into bodice, on back of waistband.

Pleats: Work with WS facing. Mark center of bound-off sts and fold bound-off sts to each side so the marker lands in the center. Sew together along the top edge and sew this to lower edge of waistband. Sew the three rem pleats the same way. Sew clasps on lower part of neckband (see page 107).

BELT

With Baby Ull Petroleum and smaller circular, CO 221 (239, 261, 295, 333) sts. Work 16 rows back and forth in stockinette. Change to larger circular. CO 5 new sts for steek (do not work steek in pattern or include in st counts). Work around in pattern fol-

lowing Chart **H**, beginning at arrow for your size. On last rnd, BO steek sts. Change to smaller circular and Baby Ull Petroleum. Work back and forth in stockinette until both facings are 3/8 in / 1 cm wider than pattern knitting. If there isn't enough Petroleum left, work facing with a different color. BO.

Reinforce steek by machine-stitching 2 lines on each side of center steek st. Carefully cut steek open up center st. **Optional:** Iron on vlieseline to WS of belt. Fold steek sts and facings to WS and sew down to cover cut edges. Sew on clasps securely.

CHART H

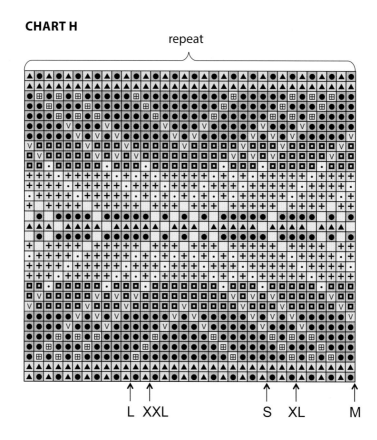

⊡	Light Pink 364	BABY ULL
V	Pastel Pink 664	ALPACA FINE
+	Coral 648	ALPACA FINE
▣	Ochre 618	ALPACA FINE
●	Cognac 653	ALPACA FINE
⊞	Light Green 631	ALPACA FINE
□	Light Blue 320	BABY ULL
▲	Petroleum 379	BABY ULL

♂CIAN PULLOVER

This long A-line sweater is named for the Irish god who ruled over the magic of love. Three moss stitch cables, framed by moss stitch, decorate the center of the body. The ribbing at lower edge has a split hem. Cian is crowned with an I-cord around the neckline.

SKILL LEVEL
Experienced

SIZES
XS (S, M, L, XL, XXL)

FINISHED MEASUREMENTS
Width: across chest, measured flat, approx. 16½ (17¾, 19, 21, 22¾, 24¾) in / 42 (45, 48, 53, 58, 63) cm; at lower edge, measured flat: approx. 19¼ (20½, 21¾, 23¾, 25½, 27½) in / 49 (52, 55, 60, 65, 70) cm
Total Length: approx. 28¼ (28¼, 29¼, 29¼, 30, 30) in / 72 (72, 74, 74, 76, 76) cm
Sleeve Length: approx. 19¼ (19¾, 19¾, 19¾, 19¾, 19¾) in / 49 (50, 50, 50, 50, 50) cm

YARN
CYCA #3 (DK, light worsted) Hillesvåg Tinde pelsull-garn (100% Norwegian wool, 284 yd/260 m / 100 g)

COLORS AND YARN AMOUNTS
Natural Gray 2115: 400 (500, 500, 500, 600, 700, 800) g

SUGGESTED NEEDLE SIZES
U. S. size 4 / 3.5 mm: straight and circular needles and set of 5 dpn; cable needle

NOTIONS
Stitch markers and tapestry needle

GAUGE
21 sts x 30 rows in stockinette = 4 x 4 in / 10 x 10 cm.
21 sts x 30 rows in moss st = 4 x 4 in / 10 x 10 cm.
Cable over 16 sts = 2¾ in / 7 cm at widest point
Adjust needle size to obtain correct gauge if necessary.

STITCHES AND TECHNIQUES
MOSS STITCH
Row 1 (RS): *K1, p1*; rep * to *.
Row 2 (WS): Work knit over knit and purl over purl.
Row 3: *P1, k1*; rep * to *.
Row 4: Work knit over knit and purl over purl.
Rep Rows 1-4.

BACK
With straight needles, CO 112 (118, 124, 134, 144, 154) sts.

Ribbing—Lower Edge
Row 1 (RS): K4 (3, 2, 3, 4, 5), (p2, k2) 6 (7, 8, 9, 10, 11) times, *(p4, k4) 2 times, p2*; rep * to * 2 more times, p2, (k2, p2) 6 (7, 8, 9, 10, 11) times, k4 (3, 2, 3, 4, 5).
Row 2 (WS): Sl 1 purlwise wyf, p3 (2, 1, 2, 3, 4), *(k2, p2), 6 (7, 8, 9, 10, 11) times, k2, *k2, (p4, k4) 2 times*; rep * to * 2 more times, *(p2, k2) 6 (7, 8, 9, 10, 11) times, p3 (2, 1, 2, 3, 4), sl 1 purlwise wyf.
Continue ribbing as est until back measures 4¼ in / 11 cm from cast-on, ending with a WS row.

Finishing the Split
Row A (RS): CO 1 st with cable cast-on method by knitting 1 st between the two outermost sts on row, place new st twisted on needle and knit it, work in ribbing as est to end of row = 113 (119, 125, 135, 145, 155) sts.
Row B (WS): CO 1 st with cable cast-on method and purl st; work in ribbing as est to end of row = 114 (120, 126, 136, 146, 156) sts.

Pattern
Row 1 (RS): K17 (20, 23, 28, 33, 38), p2, k1tbl, 8

CHART A

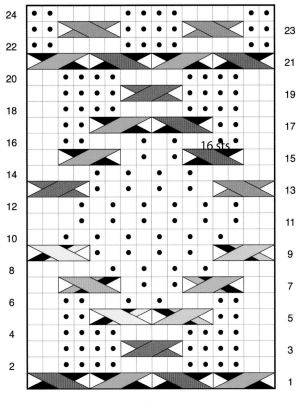

16 sts

CHART B

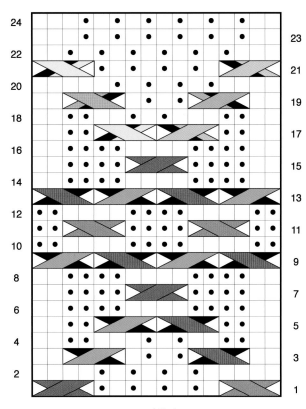

16 sts

Symbols Key

☐ Knit on RS, purl on WS

● Purl on RS, knit on WS

Sl 2 sts to cable needle and hold in back, k2; k2 from cable needle.

Sl 2 sts to cable needle and hold in front, k2; k2 from cable needle.

Sl 2 sts to cable needle and hold in back, k2; p2 from cable needle.

Sl 2 sts to cable needle and hold in front, p2; k2 from cable needle.

Sl 2 sts to cable needle and hold in back, k2; k1, p1 from cable needle.

Sl 2 sts to cable needle and hold in front, p1, k1, k2 from cable needle.

Sl 2 sts to cable needle and hold in back, k2; p1, k1 from cable needle.

Sl 2 sts to cable needle and hold in front, k1, p1, k2 from cable needle.

Symbols Key

☐ Knit on RS, purl on WS

● Purl on RS, knit on WS

Sl 2 sts to cable needle and hold in back, k2; k2 from cable needle.

Sl 2 sts to cable needle and hold in front, k2; k2 from cable needle.

Sl 2 sts to cable needle and hold in back, k2; p2 from cable needle.

Sl 2 sts to cable needle and hold in front, p2; k2 from cable needle.

Sl 2 sts to cable needle and hold in back, k2; k1, p1 from cable needle.

Sl 2 sts to cable needle and hold in front, p1, k1, k2 from cable needle.

Sl 2 sts to cable needle and hold in back, k2; p1, k1 from cable needle.

Sl 2 sts to cable needle and hold in front, k1, p1, k2 from cable needle.

sts moss, k1tbl, *p2, pm, cable over 16 sts following Chart **A**, pm, p2*, cable over 16 sts following Chart **B**, pm; rep * to * once more, k1tbl, 8 sts moss, but begin with p1, k1tbl, p2, k17 (20, 23, 28, 33, 38).

Row 2 (WS): P17 (20, 23, 28, 33, 38), k2, p1tbl, 8 sts moss, p1tbl, k2, (work charted cable up to st marker, k2) 3 times, p1tbl, 8 sts moss, p1tbl, k2, p17 (20, 23, 28, 33, 38).
Continue in pattern as est and begin shaping A-line on next row.

A-Line Shaping
Decrease Row (RS): K2, k2tog tbl, work in pattern until 4 sts rem, k2tog, k2.
Rep this decrease row on every 12th row 7 more times = total of 16 sts decreased = 98 (104, 110, 120, 130, 140) sts rem. Continue in pattern until back measures 20½ in / 52 cm from cast-on, ending with a WS row.

Shape Armholes
BO 4 (4, 4, 5, 5, 5) sts at beginning of next 2 rows.
BO 2 (3, 3, 4, 4, 4) sts at beginning of next 2 rows.
BO 1 (1, 1, 2, 3, 3) sts at beginning of next 2 (2, 4, 2, 2, 2) rows.
BO 0 (0, 0, 1, 2, 2) sts at beginning of next 0 (0, 0, 2, 2, 4) rows.
BO 0 (0, 0, 0, 1, 1) sts at beginning of next 0 (0, 0, 0, 2, 4) rows.
= 14 (16, 18, 24, 30, 36) sts decreased for armholes = 84 (88, 92, 96, 100, 104) sts rem.
Continue in pattern until armhole depth is 7 (7, 8, 8, 8¾, 8¾) in / 18 (18, 20, 20, 22, 22) cm, ending with a RS row.

Decrease Cables
Note: Decrease 4 sts in each cable rep over the back sts in cable crossing as follows:
Decrease Row (WS): Work in pattern to marker, *remove marker, work 2 sts in pattern, (work 2 sts tog in pattern) 2 times, work 4 sts in pattern (work 2 sts tog in pattern) 2 times, work 2 sts in pattern, remove marker, k2*; rep * to * 2 more times and complete row in pattern = 12 sts decreased = 72 (76, 80, 84, 88, 92) sts rem.

Right Shoulder
Next Row (RS): Work 17 (19, 19, 21, 21, 23) sts in pattern, place rem 55 (57, 61, 63, 67, 69) sts on a holder for back neck and left shoulder. Work each shoulder separately, shaping shoulder with short rows as follows:
Row 1 (WS): Work in pattern until 6 (6, 6, 7, 7, 7) sts rem, yo (bring yarn to front between the needles), sl 1 purlwise, take yarn to back of work, move st back to left needle and turn (= w&t, wrap and turn).
Row 2 (RS): Work in pattern.
Row 3: Work 6 (6, 6, 7, 7, 7) sts in pattern, yo, w&t.
Row 4: Work in pattern.
Row 5: Work in pattern across, joining each yarn-over tog tbl with the st it is wrapped around.
Place rem 17 (19, 19, 21, 21, 23) sts on a holder. Cut yarn.

Back Neck and Left Shoulder
Place held sts on needle. With RS facing, BO the center back 38 (38, 42, 42, 46, 46) sts and work 17 (19, 19, 21, 21, 23) shoulder sts as follows:
Row 1 (WS): Work in pattern until 6 (6, 6, 7, 7, 7) sts rem, yo, w&t.
Row 2 (RS): Work in pattern.
Row 3: Work 6 (6, 6, 7, 7, 7) sts in pattern, yo, w&t.
Row 4: Work in pattern.
Row 5: Work in pattern across, joining each yarn-over tog with the st it is wrapped around.
Place rem 17 (19, 19, 21, 21, 23) sts on a holder. Cut yarn.

FRONT
Work as for back until armhole depth measures 4¾ (4¾, 5½, 5½, 6¼, 6¼) in / 12 (12, 14, 14, 16, 16) cm, ending with a RS row.

Decrease Cables
Note: On WS row, decrease 4 sts in each cable rep over the back sts in cable crossing as for back = 72 (76, 80, 84, 88, 92) sts rem.

Divide for Neck
Next Row (RS): Work 22 (24, 24, 26, 26, 28) sts in pattern, place rem 50 (52, 56, 58, 62, 64) sts on a holder.

Left Side of Neck

Work 2 rows in pattern.

BO 2 sts at beginning of next WS row 2 times; BO 1 st at beginning of next WS row = 5 sts decreased for neck = 17 (19, 19, 21, 21, 23) sts rem. Continue in pattern without decreasing until armhole measures 7 (7, 8, 8, 8¾, 8¾) in / 18 (18, 20, 20, 22, 22) cm, ending with a RS row.

Left Shoulder

Work left front shoulder with short rows as for right back shoulder, beginning on a WS row.

Right Side of Neck

Attach yarn on right side and, with RS facing, BO the center 28 (28, 32, 32, 36, 36) sts for front neck; work in pattern to end of row = 22 (24, 24, 26, 26, 28) sts rem. Work 1 row on WS. BO 2 sts at beginning of next RS row 2 times, BO 1 st at beginning of next RS row = 5 sts decreased on neck edge = 17 (19, 19, 21, 21, 23) sts rem.

Continue in pattern without decreasing until armhole measures 7 (7, 8, 8, 8¾, 8¾) in / 18 (18, 20, 20, 22, 22) cm, ending with a WS row.

Right Shoulder

Work right front shoulder with short rows as for left back shoulder, beginning on 1st RS row.

SLEEVES

With straight needles, CO 48 (48, 52, 52, 56, 56) sts.

Ribbing—Cuff

Row 1 (RS): K2 (2, 4, 4, 2, 2), (p2, k2) 3 (3, 3, 3, 4, 4) times, (p4, k4) 2 times, p4, (k2, p2) 3 (3, 3, 3, 4, 4) times, k2 (2, 4, 4, 2, 2).

Row 2 (WS): P2 (2, 4, 4, 2, 2), (k2, p2) 3 (3, 3, 3, 4, 4) times, k4, (p4, k4) 2 times, (p2, k2) 3 (3, 3, 3, 4, 4) times, p2 (2, 4, 4, 2, 2).

Continue ribbing as est until cuff measures 2 in / 5 cm from cast-on, ending with a WS row.

Pattern

Row 1 (RS): K2 (2, 4, 4, 6, 6), p2, k1tbl, work 8 sts in moss st, k1tbl, p2, pm, work cable over 16 sts following Chart A, pm, p2, k1tbl, 8 sts in moss, begin-ning with p1, k1tbl, p2, k2 (2, 4, 4, 6, 6).

Row 2 (WS): P2 (2, 4, 4, 6, 6), k2, p1tbl, work 8 sts in moss st, p1tbl, k2, sl m, work cable to marker, sl m, k2, p1tbl, 8 sts in moss, p1tbl, k2, p2 (2, 4, 4, 6, 6).

Continue in pattern as est until sleeve measure 3¼ in / 8 cm from cast-on, ending with a WS row.

Increase Row (RS): K1, increase with M1, work in pattern until 1 st rem, M1, k1 = 2 sts increased = 50 (50, 54, 54, 58, 58) sts. Work new sts in stockinette. Rep the increase row every 10th (10th, 8th, 8th, 8th, 6th) row 7 (9, 9, 11, 11, 13) more times = 14 (18, 18, 22 22, 26) new sts = 64 (68, 72, 76, 80, 84) sts.

Continue in pattern without increasing until sleeve measures 19¼ (19¾, 19¾, 19¾, 19¾, 19¾) in / 49 (50, 50, 50, 50, 50) cm from cast-on or desired length, ending with a WS row.

Sleeve Cap

BO 4 (4, 4, 5, 5, 5) sts at beginning of next 2 rows = 56 (60, 64, 66, 70, 74) sts rem. Work 4 (0, 2, 2, 4, 2) rows.

BO 1 st each at beginning of next 26 (30, 32, 34, 36, 40) rows = 30 (30, 32, 32, 34, 34) sts rem.

BO 2 sts at beginning of next 2 rows = 26 (26, 28, 28, 30, 30) sts rem.

BO 3 sts at beginning of next row = 23 (23, 25, 25, 27, 27) sts rem.

Decrease Cables

Decrease Row (WS): BO 3 sts, work in pattern to marker, remove marker, work 2 sts in pattern, (work 2 sts tog in pattern) 2 times, work 4 sts in pattern (work 2 sts tog in pattern) 2 times, work 2 sts in pattern, remove marker, complete row in pattern = 7 sts decreased = 16 (16, 18, 18, 20, 20) sts rem. BO rem sts.

FINISHING

Gently steam press or block sweater to finished mea-surements if desired.

Place front and back with RS facing RS and join shoulders with three-needle bind-off.
Attach sleeves.

Seam sides down to ribbing. Seam sleeves.

Neckband
With short circular and RS facing, beginning at left shoulder, pick up and knit 17 sts along left front neck to front shaping; pick up and knit 28 (28, 32, 32, 36, 36) sts along bound-off sts; pick up and knit 17 sts along right front neck to shoulder; pick up and knit 6 sts to back neck shaping; pick up and knit 38 (38, 42, 42, 46, 46) sts along bound-off sts, pick up and knit 6 sts to left shoulder = 112 (112, 120, 120, 128, 128) sts total. Join to work in the round and pm for beginning of rnd.

Ribbing
Rnd 1: *K2, p2*; rep * to * around.
Rep Rnd 1 until neckband is approx. 1¼ in / 3 cm high. BO in ribbing.

Decorative I-Cord
To make an I-cord edging for neckband, with a small dpn and RS facing, pick up and knit sts in the first rnd of neckband and join neckband sts to cord sts as follows: Begin at left shoulder and pick up and knit 110 (110, 120, 120, 130, 130) sts In first rnd of neckband = 110 (110, 120, 120, 130, 130) sts.

CO 2 sts on left dpn, *K1, k2tog tbl, place the 2 sts back on left needle. *Do not turn*, but bring yarn firmly across back*; rep * to * to last 2 sts and leave them on needle.

Join the sts of cast-on with last 2 sts on needle with Kitchener st. Weave in all ends neatly on WS.

✦√CIAN ALPINE HAT

A moss stitch cable embellishes the brim of this alpine hat, which is a lovely accessory to match to the sweater of the same name. The ribbing holds up the crown, knitted in stockinette at the top. Designed to be worn at a jaunty angle!

SKILL LEVEL
Experienced

SIZES
Women's

FINISHED MEASUREMENTS
Circumference: approx. 21 in / 53 cm
Length: approx. 2¾ in / 7 cm

YARN
CYCA #3 (DK, light worsted) Hillesvåg Tinde pelsull-garn (100% Norwegian wool, 284 yd/260 m / 100 g)

YARN COLOR AND AMOUNT
Natural Gray 2115: 100 g

SUGGESTED NEEDLE SIZES
U. S. size 4 / 3.5 mm: circular needle and set of 5 dpn; cable needle

CROCHET HOOK
U. S. size E-4 / 3.5 mm

NOTIONS
Smooth, contrast color scrap yarn for provisional cast-on, stitch markers, and tapestry needle

GAUGE
21 sts x 30 rows in stockinette = 4 x 4 in /
10 x 10 cm.
Cable over 16 sts = 2¾ in / 7 cm at widest point.
Adjust needle size to obtain correct gauge if necessary.

Check out YouTube for various provisional cast-on methods; search for "provisional cast-on."

BRIM
With crochet hook and scrap yarn, CO 26 sts using crochet provisional cast-on method or another provisional method which allows you to release the sts to join with the bound-off edge.

RIBBING
Row 1 (RS): K3, p2, k2, p4, k4, p4, k2, p2, sl 1 wyf, k1,sl 1 wyf.
Row 2 (WS): K1, sl 1 wyf, k1tbl, k2, p2, k4, p4, k4, p2, k2, p3.
Work 2 more rows ribbing. The edge measures approx. ⅝ in / 1.5 cm from cast-on edge.

PATTERN
Note: Continue to work the 3 outermost sts on each side as est.
Row 1 (RS): Work 3 edge sts as est, p2, pm, work cable over 16 sts following Chart **A**, beginning on Row 21, pm, p2, work 3 edge sts as est.
Row 2 (WS): Work 3 edge sts as est, k2, work following chart to marker, sl m, k2, work 3 edge sts as est.
Continue in pattern, repeating Rows 1-24 on Chart **A** for moss st cable, ending on Row 2 when brim measures approx. 20½ in / 52 cm from cast-on.

RIBBED EDGE
Work 4 rows ribbing as previously. Brim should now measure approx. 21 in / 53 cm. Leave sts on needle.

FINISHING BRIM
Gently steam press or block brim to finished measurements.

117

Carefully remove scrap yarn from cast-on and place the 26 sts on a needle. Kitchener st the ends together. Weave in all ends neatly on WS.

CROWN

With RS facing and circular needle, beginning at join on brim, pick up and knit 3 sts for every 4 rows along the right edge (stockinette edge) to opposite end of brim for a total of 120 sts. Join to work in the round and pm at beginning of rnd. Purl 1 rnd.

Decrease Rnd: P4, (p2tog, p8) 11 times, p2tog, p4 = 12 sts decreased = 108 sts rem.

RIBBING

Rnd 1: *(K2, p2) 4 times, k2, pm*; rep * to * around.

Continuing in ribbing as est, increase on the next rnd:

Increase Rnd: *Rib 8 sts up to the center k2 in each marked section, M1, k2, M1, work 8 sts in pattern to marker*; rep * to * around = 12 new sts = 120 sts total.

Note: See below for how to work new sts.

Rep the increase rnd on every other rnd, working 1 st more before and after each increase, 7 more times = 84 new sts = 204 sts total. On the rnds between increase rnds, work the new sts and the k2 sts in center as follows:

Rnd 3: K4.
Rnd 5: K6.
Rnd 7: K2, p1, k2, p1, k2.
Rnd 9: (K2, p2) 2 times, k2.
Rnd 11: K2, p2, k4, p2, k2.

Rep these rnds for working new sts into ribbing. Work 3 rnds without increasing. Knit 1 rnd and then purl 3 rnds for foldline.

Change to dpn when sts no longer fit around circular. Continue in stockinette:

Next Rnd: Knit around.

There should now be 34 sts between each marker. On the next rnd, begin decreasing on each side of these 34 sts.

Decrease Rnd: *Sl 1 knitwise, sl 1 purlwise, sl the 2 sts back to left needle and k2tog tbl, knit until 2

sts before next marker, k2tog*; rep * to * around = 12 sts decreased around.

Decrease the same way on every other rnd 15 more times = 12 sts rem.

Final Decrease Rnd: *K2tog*; rep * to * around = 6 sts rem.

Cut yarn and draw end through rem sts; tighten. Weave in all ends neatly on WS.

CHART A

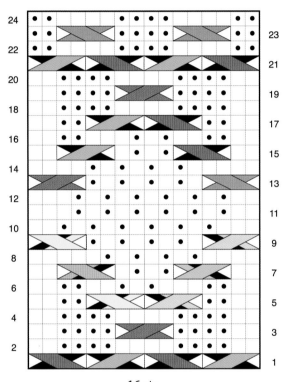

16 sts

Symbols Key

☐ Knit on RS, purl on WS

● Purl on RS, knit on WS

Sl 2 sts to cable needle and hold in back, k2; k2 from cable needle.

Sl 2 sts to cable needle and hold in front, k2; k2 from cable needle.

Sl 2 sts to cable needle and hold in back, k2; p2 from cable needle.

Sl 2 sts to cable needle and hold in front, p2; k2 from cable needle.

Sl 2 sts to cable needle and hold in back, k2; k1, p1 from cable needle.

Sl 2 sts to cable needle and hold in front, p1, k1, k2 from cable needle.

Sl 2 sts to cable needle and hold in front, k1, p1, k2 from cable needle.

Sl 2 sts to cable needle and hold in front, k1, p1, k2 from cable needle.

118

CIAN COWL

The Cian cowl is the perfect complementary touch to accompany the sweater and hat of the same name. Like a turtleneck collar, the cowl sits on top of the sweater as if part of a single piece, but can easily be removed if desired. The cowl is knitted with two moss stitch cables framed by reverse stockinette.

SKILL LEVEL
Experienced

SIZES
Women's

FINISHED MEASUREMENTS
Circumference: approx. 23¾ in / 60 cm
Length: approx. 6¾ in / 17.5 cm

YARN
CYCA #3 (DK, light worsted) Hillesvåg Tinde pelsull-garn (100% Norwegian wool, 284 yd/260 m / 100 g)

YARN COLOR AND AMOUNT
Natural Gray 2115: 100 g

SUGGESTED NEEDLE SIZE
U. S. size 4 / 3.5 mm: straight needles and cable needle

CROCHET HOOK
U. S. size E-4 / 3.5 mm

NOTIONS
Smooth, contrast color scrap yarn for provisional cast-on, stitch markers, and tapestry needle

GAUGE
21 sts x 30 rows in stockinette = 4 x 4 in / 10 x 10 cm.
Cable over 16 sts = 2¾ in / 7 cm at widest point.
Adjust needle size to obtain correct gauge if neces-sary.

COWL

With crochet hook, knitting needle, and scrap yarn, provisionally cast on 44 sts using crochet hook and knitting needle method, or another provisional method that allows you to release the sts to join with the bound-off edge.

RIBBING AND EDGING
Row 1 (RS): K1, sl 1 wyf, k1tbl, (p4, k4) 2 times, p6, (k4, p4) 2 times, sl 1 wyf, k1, sl 1 wyf.
Row 2 (WS): K1, sl 1 wyf, k1tbl, (k4, p4) 2 times, k6, (p4, k4) 2 times, sl 1 wyf, k1, sl 1 wyf.
Continue ribbing and edging as est until piece is ¾ in / 2 cm above cast-on row, ending with a WS row.

PATTERN
Note: Continue to work the 3 outermost sts on each side as est.
Row 1 (RS): Work 3 edge sts as est, (p2, pm, work cable over 16 sts following Chart **A** (see page 118), pm) 2 times, p2, work 3 edge sts as est.
Row 2 (WS): Work 3 edge sts as est, (k2, work cable following chart to marker) 2 times, k2, work 3 edge sts as est.
Continue in pattern until piece measures approx. 22¾ in / 58 cm from cast-on or desired length, end-ing with a WS row.

RIBBING AND EDGING
Work ribbing and edging as before. The piece should now measure approx. 23¾ in / 60 cm. Leave sts on needle.

FINISHING
Gently steam press or block cowl to finished mea-surements. Carefully remove scrap yarn from cast-on and place the 44 sts on a needle. Kitchener st the ends together. Weave in all ends neatly on WS.

✦ THIA CARDIGAN

This shaped cardigan has a narrow, especially sweet seed stitch rib around the waist. Cables embellish the center of the jacket and are flanked by moss stitch. The lower section of the cardigan is worked in stockinette to allow the pretty colors and depth of the hand-dyed Mikkel Rev yarn to shine. Thia finishes with a large collar that can be folded down.

SKILL LEVEL
Experienced

SIZES
XS (S, M, L, XL, XXL)

FINISHED MEASUREMENTS
Half Width: excluding front bands, measured flat, approx. 16½ (17¾, 19, 21, 22¾, 24¾) in / 42 (45, 48, 53, 58, 63) cm; at waist, measured flat, approx. 15 (16¼, 17¼, 19¼, 21¼, 23¼) in / 38 (41, 44, 49, 54, 59) cm; at lower edge, measured flat: approx. 17¼ (18½, 19¾, 21¾, 23¾, 25½) in / 44 (47, 50, 55, 60, 65) cm
Total Length: approx. 24 (24½, 24¾, 25¼, 25½, 26) in / 61 (62, 63, 64, 65, 66) cm
Sleeve Length: approx. 19¼ (19¾, 19¾, 19¾, 19¾, 19¾) in / 49 (50, 50, 50, 50, 50) cm

YARN
CYCA #3 (DK, light worsted) Mikkel Rev dyed on Hillesvåg Tinde pelsullgarn (100% Norwegian wool, 284 yd/260 m / 100 g). Dyed yarn available from Værbitt Garn, www.varbitt.no

YARN COLOR AND AMOUNT
Weathered, Mikkel Rev: 400 (500, 500, 600, 700, 800) g

SUGGESTED NEEDLE SIZES
U. S. size 4 / 3.5 mm: straight needles, circular (you'll need an extra circular for joins and welts), and set of 5 dpn
U.S. size 2.5 / 3 mm: short and long circulars; cable needle

NOTIONS
11 buttons, stitch markers, and tapestry needle

GAUGE
21 sts x 30 rows in stockinette on larger needles = 4 x 4 in / 10 x 10 cm.
21 sts x 30 rows in seed st ribbing on larger needles = 4 x 4 in / 10 x 10 cm.
21 sts x 30 rows in moss st on larger needles = 4 x 4 in / 10 x 10 cm.
Adjust needle size to obtain correct gauge if necessary.
Cable over 12 sts = approx. 2 in / 5 cm.

GARMENT CONSTRUCTION
The jacket is worked in pieces and then sewn together. Each garment piece is worked in two parts which are knitted together as you work. The seed stitch ribbing is not joined at the sides in the lower section.

STITCHES AND TECHNIQUES

SEED STITCH RIBBING (MULTIPLE OF 4 + 3 STS)
Row 1 (RS): *K3, p1*; rep * to * until 3 sts rem, end k3.
Row 2 (WS): K1, p1, *K3, p1*; rep * to * until 1 st rem, end k1.
Rep Rows 1-2.

MOSS STITCH
Row 1 (RS): *K1, p1*; rep * to *.
Row 2 (WS): Work knit over knit and purl over purl.
Row 3: *P1, k1*; rep * to *.
Row 4: Work knit over knit and purl over purl.
Rep Rows 1-4 for pattern.

LOWER BACK

With larger circular, CO 95 (99, 107, 115, 127, 139) sts.

Seed Stitch Ribbing

Beginning on RS, work all sts across in seed st ribbing until piece measures approx. 2¾ in / 7 cm from cast-on row. End with a WS row.

Set-up Row (RS): K47 (49, 53, 57, 63, 69), M1, k48 (50, 54, 58, 64, 70) = 96 (100, 108, 116, 128, 140) sts.

Stockinette

Continue in stockinette; the first row is on WS. Begin waist shaping on the next row (see below). When back measures approx. 3 in / 7.5 cm from cast-on, end with a WS row.

Waist

Decrease Row (RS): K1, k2tog tbl, work in stockinette until 3 sts rem, k2tog, k1 = 2 sts decreased.
Rep decrease row every 6th row 6 (3, 6, 3, 3, 6) more times and then on every 8th row 0 (2, 0, 2, 2, 0) times = 82 (88, 94, 104, 116, 126) sts rem. Continue in stockinette without decreasing until lower back measures 9¼ in / 23.5 cm from cast-on, ending with a WS row.

Increase Row (RS): K1, M1, work in stockinette until 1 st rem, M1, k1 = 2 sts increased.
Rep increase row every 6th row 3 more times = 90 (96, 102, 112, 124, 134) sts. End with a WS row and then continue in stockinette without increasing until lower back measures 11¾ in / 30 cm from cast-on, ending with a RS row.

Sizes XS (M, 2XL) only:

Increase Row (WS): P45 (51, 67), M1p, p45 (51, 67) = 91 (103, 135) sts.

Sizes S (L, XL) only:

Decrease Row (WS): P47 (55, 61), p2tog, p47 (55, 61) = 95 (111, 123) sts.

All sizes:

Place sts on a holder; cut yarn.

UPPER BACK

With larger circular, CO 91 (95, 103, 111, 123, 135) sts.

Seed Stitch Ribbing

Beginning on RS, work all sts across in seed st ribbing until piece measures approx. 1½ in / 4 cm from cast-on row. End with a WS row. Do not cut yarn.

JOINING LOWER AND UPPER BACK PIECES

Place the upper back over lower back, with both pieces facing you. Begin on RS. Using an extra larger size needle and yarn from upper back, k2tog across, joining 1 st from each piece for each join.

Note: All measurements are now taken from cast-on row of lower back.

WELT

Using an extra larger circular, hold both needles parallel in your right hand, purl every st of each needle across. Slide sts on to cable of circular. Let sts rest until welt is finished. Knit across. Work 4 more rows in stockinette.

Close welt as follows: Fold welt so that you are holding the extra circular behind work and p2tog across with 1 st from each needle for each join.

Pattern

Row 1 (RS): K13 (15, 19, 23, 29, 35), p2, k1tbl, 8 sts moss st, k1tbl, p2, *pm, k4, M1, k7, pm*; p2, pm, k7, M1, k4, pm, p2; rep * to * once. P2, k1tbl, 8 sts moss st beginning with p1, k1tbl, p2, k13 (15, 19, 23, 29, 35) = 3 sts increased = 94 (98, 106, 114, 126, 138) sts.
Row 2: (WS): P13 (15, 19, 23, 29, 35), k2, p1tbl, 8 sts moss st, p1tbl, k2, *work cable 1 over 12 sts following Chart **A** (beginning on Row 2)*, k2, work cable 2 over 12 sts following Chart **B** (beginning on Row 2), k2; rep from * to * 1 time, k2, p1tbl, 8 sts moss st, p1tbl, k2, p13 (15, 19, 23, 29, 35).

On next row, begin increasing, *at the same time* as continuing in pattern, repeating Rows 1-8 of cable charts.

CHART A

Cable 1

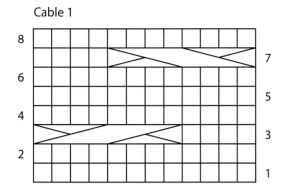

CHART B

Cable 2

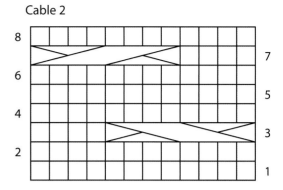

 Knit on RS, purl on WS

Sl 4 sts to cable needle and hold in front, k4, k4 from cable needle.

Sl 4 sts to cable needle and hold in back, k4, k4 from cable needle.

Increase Row (RS): K1, M1, work in pattern until 1 st rem, M1, k1 = 2 sts increased.

Rep increase row on every 6th (8th, 6th, 8th, 8th, 6th) row 2 more times = 100 (104, 112, 120, 132, 144) sts. Continue in pattern until back measures 16½ in / 42 cm from lower back cast-on, ending with WS row.

Shape Armholes
BO 4 (4, 4, 4, 5, 5) sts at beginning of next two rows. At beginning of next 4 (0, 2, 2, 2, 2) rows, BO 1 (1, 2, 3, 4, 4) sts.
BO 0 (0, 1, 2, 2, 3) sts at beginning of next 0 (0, 4, 2, 4, 2) rows.
At beginning of next 0 (0, 0, 2, 2, 4) rows, BO 0 (0, 0, 1, 1, 2) sts.
BO 0 (0, 0, 0, 0, 1) sts at beginning of next 0 (0, 0, 0, 0, 4) rows = 12 (12, 16, 20, 28, 36) sts decreased for armholes = 88 (92, 96, 100, 104, 108) sts rem. Continue without further shaping until armhole depth measures 6¾ (7, 7½, 8, 8¼, 8¾) in / 17 (18, 19, 20, 21, 22) cm, ending with a RS row.

Decreasing Cables
Decrease Row (WS): Work in pattern to marker, *remove marker, (p2tog) 2 times, p4, (p2tog) 2 times, remove marker, k2*; rep * to * 2 more times, work in pattern to end of row = 12 sts decreased = 76 (80, 84, 88, 92, 96) sts rem.

Right Shoulder
Next Row (RS): Work 20 (22, 23, 24, 25, 25) sts in pattern, place rem 56 (58, 61, 64, 67, 71) sts on a holder for back neck and left shoulder. Continue in short rows as follows:
Row 1 (WS): Work in pattern until 7 (7, 8, 8, 9, 9) sts rem, yo (bring yarn to front between needles), sl 1 purlwise, take yarn to back; turn = w&t (wrap and turn).
Row 2 (RS): Work across in pattern.
Row 3: Work 6 (6, 7, 7, 8, 8) sts in pattern, yo, w&t.
Row 4: Work across in pattern.

Row 5: Work across in pattern, purling each yarn-over tbl with the st it wraps. Place sts on a holder; cut yarn.

Back Neck and Left Shoulder
On RS, attach yarn and place the 56 (58, 61, 64, 67, 71) held sts on larger needles. BO the center back 36 (36, 38, 40, 42, 46) sts for back neck and work rem 20 (22, 23, 24, 25, 25) sts for shoulder. Work in short rows as follows:
Row 1 (RS): Work in pattern until 7 (7, 8, 8, 9, 9) sts rem, yo, w&t.
Row 2 (WS): Work across in pattern.
Row 3: Work 6 (6, 7, 7, 8, 8) sts in pattern, yo, w&t.
Row 4: Work across in pattern.
Row 5: Work across in pattern, knitting each yarn-over with the st it wraps.
Work next row (WS) in pattern. Place sts on a holder; cut yarn.

LOWER LEFT FRONT
With larger circular, CO 47 (47, 51, 55, 59, 67) sts.

Seed Stitch Ribbing
Beginning on RS, work all sts across in seed st ribbing until piece measures approx. 2¾ in / 7 cm from cast-on row. End with a WS row.

Set-up Row (RS): K22 (22, 24, 27, 29, 33), k2tog, k23 (23, 25, 26, 28, 32) = 46 (46, 50, 54, 58, 66) sts.

Stockinette
Continue in stockinette; the first row is on WS. Begin waist shaping on the next row (see below). When lower left front measures approx. 3 in / 7.5 cm from cast-on, end with a WS row.

Waist
Decrease Row (RS): K1, k2tog tbl, knit to end of row = 45 (45, 49, 53, 57, 65) sts.
Rep decrease row every 6th row 6 (3, 6, 3, 3, 6) more times and then on every 8th row 0 (2, 0, 2, 2, 0) times = 39 (40, 43, 48, 52, 59) sts rem.

Continue in stockinette without decreasing until lower left front measures 9¼ in / 23.5 cm from cast-on, ending with a WS row.

Increase Row (RS): K1, M1, Knit to end of row = 40 (41, 44, 49, 53, 60) sts.

Rep increase row every 6th row 3 (2, 3, 2, 2, 3) more times = 43 (43, 47, 51, 55, 63) sts. End with a WS purl row.

Sizes S (L, XL) only:
Work 6 rows in stockinette without increasing. The lower left front should now measure approx. 11¾ in / 30 cm from cast-on. End with a RS row.

Place sts on an extra larger circular. Cut yarn.

UPPER LEFT FRONT
With larger circular, CO 43 (43, 47, 51, 55, 63) sts.

Seed Stitch Ribbing
Beginning on RS, work all sts across in seed st ribbing until piece measures approx. 1½ in / 4 cm from cast-on row. End with a WS row.

JOINING LOWER AND UPPER LEFT FRONT PIECES
Place the upper left front over lower left front, with both pieces facing you.
Begin on RS with yarn from upper left front, k2tog across, joining 1 st from each piece for each join.

WELT
Using an extra larger circular, hold both needles parellel in your right hand and purl every st of each needle across. Slide sts on to cable of circular. Let sts rest until welt is finished. Knit across. Work 4 more rows in stockinette.

Close welt as follows: Fold welt so that you are holding the extra circular behind work and p2tog across with 1 st from each needle for each join.

Pattern
Row 1 (RS): K13 (15, 19, 23, 28, 34), p2, k1tbl, 8 sts moss st, k1tbl, p2, pm, k6, (M1, k1) 0 (2, 2, 2, 3, 1) times, k6 (2, 2, 2, 0, 4), pm, p2, k1tbl, k1 = 43 (45, 49, 53, 58, 64) sts.
Row 2: (WS): P1, p1tbl, k2, work cable 1 over 12 sts following Chart **A** (beginning on Row 2), k2, p1tbl, 8 sts moss st, p1tbl, k2, p13 (15, 19, 23, 28, 34).
Continue in pattern and begin increasing on next row.

Increase Row (RS): K1, M1, work in pattern to end of row = 44 (46, 50, 54, 59, 65) sts.
Rep increase row on every 6th (8th, 6th, 8th, 8th, 6th) row 2 (2, 2, 3, 3, 2) more times = 46 (48, 52, 57, 62, 67) sts.

Continue in pattern until front measures 16½ in / 42 cm from lower left front cast-on, ending with WS row.

Shape Armhole
BO 4 (4, 4, 4, 5, 5) sts at beginning of next RS row.
BO 1 (1, 2, 3, 4, 4) sts at beginning of next RS row 2 (2, 1, 1, 1, 1) times.
BO 0 (0, 1, 2, 2, 3) sts at beginning of next RS row 0 (0, 2, 1, 2, 1) times.
BO 0 (0, 0, 1, 1, 2) sts at beginning of next RS row 0 (0, 0, 1, 1, 2) times.
BO 0 (0, 0, 0, 0, 1) sts at beginning of next RS row 0 (0, 0, 0, 0, 2) times = 6 (6, 8, 11, 14, 18) sts decreased for armhole = 40 (42, 44, 46, 48, 49) sts rem.
Continue without further shaping until armhole depth measures 4 (4½, 5, 5¼, 5¾, 6) in / 10.5 (11.5 12.5, 13.5, 14.5, 15.5) cm, ending with a RS row.

Decreasing Cables
Decrease Row (WS): Work in pattern to marker, remove marker; (p2tog) 2 times, p4, (p2tog) 2 times, remove marker; work in pattern to end of row = 4 sts decreased = 36 (38, 40, 42, 44, 45) sts rem.

Work 1 row on RS, working cable sts as sts face you.

Neck
Next Row (WS): BO (11, 12, 13, 14, 15) sts, work in pattern to end of row = 25 (27, 28, 29, 30, 30) sts rem.
Continue shaping neck: BO 3 sts at beginning of next WS row, and then 1 st at beginning of next WS row 2 times = 20 (22, 23, 24, 25, 25) sts rem.

Continue without further shaping until armhole depth measures 6¾ (7, 7½, 8, 8¼, 8¾) in / 17 (18, 19, 20, 21, 22) cm, ending with a RS row.

Shoulder
Shape shoulder with short rows as for right back shoulder.

LOWER RIGHT FRONT
Work as for lower left front to waist.

Waist
Decrease Row (RS): Knit until 3 sts rem, k2tog, k1 = 45 (45, 49, 53, 57, 65) sts.

Rep decrease row every 6th row 6 (3, 6, 3, 3, 6) more times and then on every 8th row 0 (2, 0, 2, 2, 0) times = 39 (40, 43, 48, 52, 59) sts rem.

Continue in stockinette without decreasing until lower right front measures 9¼ in / 23.5 cm from cast-on, ending with a WS row.

Increase Row (RS): Knit until 1 st rem, M1, k1 = 40 (41, 44, 49, 53, 60) sts.

Rep increase row every 6th row 3 (2, 3, 2, 2, 3) more times = 43 (43, 47, 51, 55, 63) sts. End with a WS purl row.

Sizes S (L, XL) only:
Work 6 rows in stockinette without increasing. The lower right front should now measure approx. 11¾ in / 30 cm from cast-on. End with a RS row.

Place sts on an extra larger circular. Cut yarn.

UPPER RIGHT FRONT
Work as for upper left front.

JOINING LOWER AND UPPER RIGHT FRONT PIECES
Join pieces in pattern as for lower and upper left front = 43 (43, 47, 51, 55, 63) sts.

Pattern
Row 1 (RS): K1, k1tbl, p2, pm, k6 (2, 2, 2, 0, 4), (M1, k1) 0 (2, 2, 2, 3, 1) times, k6, pm, p2, k1tbl, 8 sts double seed st, k1tbl, p2, k13 (15, 19, 23, 28, 34) = 43 (45, 49, 53, 58, 64) sts.

Row 2: (WS): P13 (15, 19, 23, 28, 34), k2, p1tbl, 8 sts double seed, p1tbl, k2, work cable 2 over 12 sts following Chart **B** (beginning on Row 2), k2, p1tbl, p1.

Continue in pattern and begin increasing on next row.

Increase Row (RS): Work in pattern until 1 st rem, M1, k1 = 44 (46, 50, 54, 59, 65) sts.

Rep increase row on every 6th (8th, 6th, 8th, 8th, 6th) row 2 (2, 2, 3, 3, 2 more times = 46 (48, 52, 57, 62, 67) sts.

Continue in pattern until front measures 16½ in / 42 cm from lower right front cast-on, ending with WS row.

Shape Armhole
BO 4 (4, 4, 4, 5, 5) sts at beginning of next WS row.
BO 1 (1, 2, 3, 4, 4) sts at beginning of next WS row 2 (2, 1, 1, 1, 1) times.
BO 0 (0, 1, 2, 2, 3) sts at beginning of next WS row 0 (0, 2, 1, 2, 1) times.
BO 0 (0, 0, 1, 1, 2) sts at beginning of next WS row 0 (0, 0, 1, 1, 2) times.
BO 0 (0, 0, 0, 0, 1) sts at beginning of next WS row 0 (0, 0, 0, 0, 2) times = 6 (6, 8, 11, 14, 18) sts decreased for armholes = 40 (42, 44, 46, 48, 49) sts rem.
Continue without further shaping until armhole depth measures 4 (4½, 5, 5¼, 5¾, 6) in / 10.5 (11.5 12.5, 13.5, 14.5, 15.5) cm, ending with a RS row.

Decreasing Cables
Decrease Row (WS): Work in pattern to marker, remove marker, (p2tog) 2 times, p4, (p2tog) 2 times, remove marker, work in pattern to end of row = 4 sts decreased = 36 (38, 40, 42, 44, 45) sts rem.

Neck
Next Row (RS): BO (11, 12, 13, 14, 15) sts, work in pattern to end of row = 25 (27, 28, 29, 30, 30) sts rem.
Continue shaping neck: BO 3 sts at beginning of next RS row, and then 1 st at beginning of next RS row 2 times = 20 (22, 23, 24, 25, 25) sts rem.

Continue without further shaping until armhole depth measures 6¾ (7, 7½, 8, 8¼, 8¾) in / 17 (18, 19, 20, 21, 22) cm, ending with a WS row.

Shoulder
Shape shoulder with short rows as for left back shoulder.

SLEEVES
With larger circular, CO 43 (43, 47, 47, 51, 51) sts.

Seed Stitch Ribbing
Beginning on RS, work all sts across in seed st ribbing until piece measures approx. 2 in / 5 cm from cast-on row. End with a RS row.

Set-up Row (WS): Work 22 (22, 24, 24, 26, 26) in seed st ribbing, (M1p, 1 st in pattern) 5 times, work 16 (16, 18,18, 20, 20) sts in seed st ribbing = 48 (48, 52, 52, 56, 56) sts.

Pattern
Row 1 (RS): K4 (4, 6, 6, 8, 8), p2, k1tbl, 8 sts moss st, k1tbl, p2, pm, work cable 1 over 12 sts following Chart **A**, pm, p2, k1tbl, 8 sts moss st, k1tbl, p2, k4 (4, 6, 6, 8, 8).
Row 2: (WS): P4 (4, 6, 6, 8, 8), k2, p1tbl, 8 sts moss st, p1tbl, k2, work 12 sts following Chart **A**, k2, p1tbl, 8 sts moss st, p1tbl, k2, p4 (4, 6, 6, 8, 8).
Continue in pattern until sleeve is 3¼ in above cast-on row, ending on WS row.

Increase Row (RS): K1, M1, work in pattern until 1 st rem, M1, k1 = 50 (50, 54, 54, 58, 58) sts.
Rep increase row every 10th (10th, 8th, 8th, 8th, 6th) row 7 (9, 9, 11, 11, 13) more times. Work new sts in stockinette = 64 (68, 72, 76, 80, 84) sts.

Continue in pattern without further increasing until sleeve measures 19¼ (19¾, 19¾, 19¾, 19¾, 19¾) in / 49 (50, 50, 50, 50, 50) cm or desired length, ending on a WS row.

Sleeve Cap
At beginning of next 2 rows, BO 4 (4, 4, 5, 5, 5) sts = 56 (60, 64, 66, 70, 74) sts rem.
Work 4 (0, 2, 2, 4, 0) rows.

At beginning of next 26 (30, 32, 34, 36, 36) rows, BO
1 st = 30 (30, 32, 32, 34, 38) sts rem.
BO 2 sts at beginning of next 2 (2, 2, 2, 4) rows =
26 (26, 28, 28, 30, 30) sts rem.
BO 3 sts at beginning of next row = 23 (23, 25, 25,
27, 27 sts rem.

Decreasing Cables
Decrease Row (WS): BO 3 sts, work in pattern to
marker, remove marker, p2tog, p2, (p2tog) 2 times,
p2, p2tog, remove maker, work in pattern to end of
row = 7 sts decreased = 16 (16, 18, 18, 20, 20) sts
rem. Loosely BO rem sts.

FINISHING
Gently steam press or block pieces out to finished
measurements if desired. With RS facing RS, join
shoulders with 3-needle BO.

Collar
With RS facing and larger circular, pick up and knit
sts along edge. Begin at right front and to shoulder,
pick up and knit 36 (37, 37, 38, 38, 39) sts (or pick up
and knit 3 sts for every 4 rows), pick up and knit 47
(49, 49, 51, 51, 53) sts across back, pick up and knit
36 (37, 37, 38, 38, 39) sts along left front = 119 (123,
123, 127, 127) sts total.
Row 1 (WS): P2, *k3, p1*; rep * to * until 1 st rem,
end p1.
Row 2 (RS): *K3, p1*; rep * to * until 3 sts rem, end
k3.
Continue in seed st ribbing until collar measures 6¼
in / 16 cm, ending with a WS row.
BO in seed st ribbing.

Right Front Band
With RS facing and smaller circular, pick up and
knit sts along front edge. Begin at lower edge of
right front, and, to beginning of upper front, pick up
and knit 59 sts, pick up and knit 58 (60, 62, 64, 66,
68) sts to collar, pick up and knit 35 sts along collar
= 152 (154, 156, 158, 160, 162) sts total.
Row 1 (WS): Purl.
Row 2 (RS, buttonhole row): K6 (8, 10, 10, 10, 10),
BO 2 sts, (k12, BO 2 sts) 0 (0, 0, 2, 4, 6) times, (k11,
BO 2 sts) 10 (10, 10, 8, 6, 4) times, k14 = 11 buttonholes.
Row 3: *Purl to gap, turn so RS faces you, CO 1 st by
knitting between the last 2 sts, place st back on left
needle, begin to CO 1 st more (= knit between the
last 2 sts but turn st when placing it on left needle;
tug so yarn between the two needles goes to RS,
place new st on left needle; turn to WS*; rep * to *
10 times more, purl to end of row.
Rows 4 and 6: Knit.
Row 5: Knit on WS for foldline.
Row 7: Purl.
Row 8: Work as for Row 2.
Row 9: Work as for Row 3.
BO. Fold band along 5th row and sew down on WS
with outermost st loop of picked up st edge.

Left Front Band
Work as for right front band, omitting buttonholes
(knit Rows 2 and 8, purl Rows 3 and 9).

Sew buttons to left front band to match buttonholes.
Seam sides and sleeves. Weave in all ends neatly on
WS.

DAMARA SKIRT

This asymmetrical skirt, named for a goddess of fertility, has a checkerboard rib pattern. The high ribbed waist is relaxed, so the skirt can hang on your hips or be folded down. Both styles use a belt to hold it up. Damara is knitted in pieces with a side seam. The ribbing is worked last so you can easily adjust it to your own measurements. The skirt can also be worn as a poncho.

SKILL LEVEL
Experienced

SIZES
XS/S (M/L, XL/XXL)

FINISHED MEASUREMENTS
Ribbing at Waist: approx. 27½ (32¼, 37) in / 70 (82, 94) cm
Width: at hip, approx. 30 (36¼, 41¾) in / 76 (92, 106) cm; at lower edge: approx. 43¾ (47¼, 51½) in / 111 (120, 131) cm
Total Length: excluding ribbing, approx. 21¾ (22½, 23¼) in / 55 (57, 59) cm
Ribbing Length: approx. 6 in / 15 cm

YARN
CYCA #3 (DK, light worsted), Hillesvåg Tinde pelsull-garn (100% Norwegian wool, 284 yd/260 m / 100 g)

YARN COLOR AND AMOUNTS
Burgundy 2104: 400 (500, 600) g

SUGGESTED NEEDLE SIZE
U. S. size 4 / 3.5 mm: short and long circulars

CROCHET HOOK
U.S. size E-4 / 3.5 mm for provisional cast-on

NOTIONS
Stitch markers, tapestry needle, and smooth, contrast color scrap yarn

GAUGE
21 sts x 30 rows in stockinette = 4 x 4 in / 10 x 10 cm.
21 sts x 30 rows in seed st ribbing in checkerboard pattern = 4 x 4 in / 10 x 10 cm.
20 sts x 30 rows in ribbing = 4 x 4 in / 10 x 10 cm.
Adjust needle size to obtain correct gauge if necessary.

GARMENT CONSTRUCTION

The skirt is made out of two identical pieces, from the top down. It begins with a provisional cast-on, which is removed later after the side seam is sewn (or crocheted) together. Finally, the ribbing at the top is worked in the round. The ribbing is very elastic so that the skirt can be pulled up or down as you wish and it is held in place with a belt.

BACK

Using scrap yarn and long circular, CO 83 (97, 113) sts with a provisional cast-on. For example, you can try the crochet provisional cast-on with chain sts worked around a knitting needle. End with 5 extra chain sts and then cut scrap yarn. Change to Burgundy Tinde Pelsullgarn.

TIP
For a video of the crochet cast-on, check YouTube, searching for "provisional crochet cast-on."

Pattern

Row 1 (RS): K0 (1, 0), work 83 (95, 113) sts in seed st ribbing in checkerboard pattern following Chart A, k0 (1, 0).

Row 2 (WS): P0 (1, 0), work in pattern until 0 (1, 0) sts rem, end p0 (1, 0).

Continue in pattern until back measures 1¼ in / 3 cm from cast-on.

Shaping

Increase Row (RS): K1, 1 st in pattern, M1, work in pattern until 2 sts rem, M1, 1 st in pattern, k1 = 2 sts increased = 85 (99, 115) sts.

Rep increase row on every RS row 74 (77, 80) times, working all new sts into pattern = 148 (154, 160) sts increased = 233 (253, 275) sts.

Work 6 (6, 10) rows in pattern without increasing = ¾ (¾, 1³/₈) in / 2 (2, 3.5) cm. The back should now measure 21¾ (22½, 23¼) in / 55 (57, 59) cm above cast-on. BO in pattern using a very elastic bind-off method by twisting the right needle clockwise before a knit st and counter-clockwise before a purl st.

CHART A

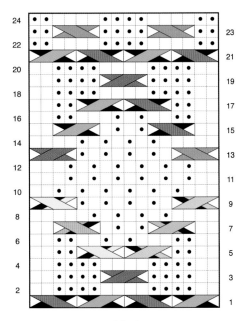

16 sts

TIP

For a video of the elastic bind-off, check YouTube, searching for "elastic bind-off."

FRONT

Work as for back.

FINISHING

Gently steam press or block pieces out to finished measurements if desired.

Seam sides up to the provisional cast-on.

RIBBING

Carefully remove scrap yarn in provisional cast-on and, with RS facing, place 83 (97, 113) sts of front and 83 (97, 113) sts of back on short circular = 166 (194, 226) sts total.

Join and work in the round; pm for beginning of rnd.

Decrease Rnd: K2 (3, 2), k2tog, k5 (6, 4), (k2tog) 10 (11, 33) times, k4 (5, 3), (k2tog) 15 (14, 4) times, k2 (3, 4) = 26 (26, 38) sts decreased = 140 (168, 188) sts rem.

Ribbing Rnd: *K2, p2*; rep * to * around.

Continue in ribbing until piece measures 6 in / 15 cm or desired length.

BO in ribbing using the very elastic bind-off method by twisting the right needle clockwise before a knit st and counter-clockwise before a purl st. Weave in all ends neatly on WS.

Symbols Key

☐ Knit on RS, purl on WS

● Purl on RS, knit on WS

Sl 2 sts to cable needle and hold in back, k2; k2 from cable needle.

Sl 2 sts to cable needle and hold in front, k2; k2 from cable needle.

Sl 2 sts to cable needle and hold in back, k2; p2 from cable needle.

Sl 2 sts to cable needle and hold in front, p2; k2 from cable needle.

Sl 2 sts to cable needle and hold in back, k2; k1, p1 from cable needle.

Sl 2 sts to cable needle and hold in front, p1, k1, k2 from cable needle.

Sl 2 sts to cable needle and hold in front, k1, p1, k2 from cable needle.

Sl 2 sts to cable needle and hold in front, k1, p1, k2 from cable needle.

CHECKERBOARD BEADED RIB

1 repeat = 4 sts

☐ Knit on RS, purl on WS

● Purl on RS, knit on WS

☐ Pattern repeat

HANNAH PULLOVER

For this pullover, I worked with a technique in which the main color is knitted and the pattern color is purled. That breaks up the pattern, with the purl stitches producing a relief effect, for a look that reminds me of weaving and embroidery. The sweater has waist shaping and inset sleeves that are knitted together with the body in the yoke. The only sewing you'll have to do is seaming the shoulders and sleeve tops.

SKILL LEVEL
Experienced

SIZES
XS (S, M, L, XL)

FINISHED MEASUREMENTS
Chest: approx. 34¾ (37¾, 41, 44, 47¼) in / 88 (96, 104, 112, 120) cm
Total Length: approx. 23¾ (24½, 25¼, 26, 26¾) in / 60 (62, 64, 66, 68) cm
Sleeve Length: approx. 18½ (19, 19¼, 19¾, 20) in / 47 (48, 49, 50, 51) cm

YARN
CYCA #3 (DK, light worsted) Du Store Alpakka Sterk (40% finest alpaca, 40% Merino wool, 20% nylon, 150 yd/137 m / 50 g)
CYCA #1 (fingering) Du Store Alpakka Alpakka Wool (60% finest alpaca, 40% pure new wool, 182 yd/166 m / 50 g)

YARN COLORS AND AMOUNTS
Color 1: Sterk Light Beige Heather 845: 350 (350, 400, 450, 500) g
Color 2: Alpakka Wool Charcoal Gray Heather 504: 200 (200, 250, 250, 300) g

SUGGESTED NEEDLE SIZES
U. S. sizes 1.5 and 2.5 / 2.5 and 3 mm: long and short circulars and sets of 5 dpn

GAUGE
26 sts x 30 rnds in pattern on larger needles = 4 x 4 in / 10 x 10 cm.
Adjust needle size to obtain correct gauge if necessary.

STITCHES AND TECHNIQUES

SEED STITCH IN THE ROUND
Rnd 1: *K1, p1*; rep * to * around.
Rnd 2: *P1, k1*; rep * to *around
Rep Rnds 1-2.

2-COLOR PATTERN IN KNIT AND PURL
Color 1 is worked in stockinette and Color 2 is purled throughout. Make sure that Color 2 lies on the back of the work as you knit. When there are long floats between colors, twist the colors around each other on WS every 4 or 5 stitches. Also, be careful not to stack the color twists to prevent the colors showing through on RS.

BODY

With Color 1 and smaller circular, CO 230 (250, 270, 290, 310) sts. Join, being careful not to twist cast-on row; pm for beginning of rnd. Knit 1 rnd. Continue in **seed st in the round:** *Work Rnd 1 with Color 1, and Rnd 2 with Color 2*; rep * to * 3 more times. Knit 1 rnd with Color 1. Change to larger circular and pm at each side with 115 (125, 135, 145, 155) sts each for front and back. Knit 1 rnd and then continue in pattern following chart. Begin at arrow for your size, knit to next side marker and then begin again at same arrow.

Note: When piece measures 4 (4¼, 4¾, 5¼, 5½) in / 10 (11, 12, 13, 14) cm, decrease 1 st at each side of each marker. Decrease the same way every ¾ (1, 1, 1¼, 1¼) in / 2 (2.5, 2.5, 3, 3) cm. Decrease with k2tog tbl (or ssk) before each marker and k2tog after each marker. Decrease a total of 4 times = 107 (117, 127, 137, 147) sts rem each for front and back.

Continue in pattern until piece measures 8 (8¾, 9½, 10¼, 11) in / 20 (22, 24, 26, 28) cm. Now increase 1 st with M1 on each side of each marker. Increase a total of 4 times = 115 (125, 135, 145, 155) sts each for front and back. Continue in pattern until body measures 16¼ (16½, 17, 17¼, 17¾) in / 41 (42, 43, 44, 45) cm. BO 10 sts on each side for armholes (= BO 5 sts on each side of each marker) = 105 (115, 125, 135, 145) sts rem each for front and back. Set body aside while you knit sleeves.

SLEEVES
With Color 1 and smaller dpn, CO 59 (61, 63, 65, 67) sts. Divide sts onto 4 dpn and join, being careful not to twist cast-on row; pm for beginning of rnd. Knit 1 rnd. Continue in **seed st in the round:** *Work Rnd 1 with Color 1, and Rnd 2 with Color 2*; rep * to * 3 more times. Knit 2 rnds with Color 1. Change to larger dpn and work in pattern following chart, beginning on **Row 41 of char**t, at arrow or your size. Pm at center of underarm. Increase 1 st with M1 on each side of marker every ¾ (¾, ¾, ⅝, ⅝) in / 2 (2, 2, 1.5, 1.5) cm a total of 20 (22, 23, 25, 26) times = 99 (105, 109, 115, 119) sts. Continue in pattern until sleeve is 18½ (19, 19¼, 19¾, 20) in / 47 (48, 49, 50, 51) cm long.

Note: Make sure that last pattern rnd on sleeve is the same as on the body.

BO 10 sts on centered on underarm (= BO 5 sts on each side of marker) = 89 (95, 99, 105, 109) sts rem. Make the second sleeve the same way.

YOKE
Place all the pieces on larger circular as follows: one sleeve, front, second sleeve, and back = 388 (420, 448, 480, 508) sts total. Pm around 1 st at each intersection of sleeve and body (= pm in first and last sts of each sleeve). Continue in pattern, making sure

that the center st is centered on each sleeve, front, and back. The center st is always knitted in the MC. *At the same time*, on Rnd 2, begin shaping armholes and sleeve caps: K2tog tbl (or ssk) before each marked st and k2tog after each marked st. Work marked st in Color 1.

BO on front and back: 1 st at each side, on every rnd 3 (6, 8, 10, 12) times and then on every other rnd 3 (3, 4, 5, 6) times = 93 (97, 101, 105, 109) sts rem each for front and back. *At the same time*, **BO on sleeves:** 1 st at each side, on every rnd 8 times (all sizes), and then on every other rnd 14 (15, 17, 18, 20) times, and finally, on every rnd 7 (8, 7, 8, 7) times = 31 (33, 35, 37, 39) sts rem on each sleeve.

On next rnd, BO the center front 27 (29, 29, 31, 31) sts for neck and, *at the same time*, BO 29 (31, 33, 35, 37) sts over each sleeve. The 1 st that rem on each side of each sleeve will now be worked as edge sts for front and back.

Now work front and back separately.

BACK
= 93 (97, 101, 105, 109) sts. Continue in pattern, working back and forth to finished length.

Note: Make sure the Color 2 is purled on RS.

When back is approx. 1½ (1½, 1½, 2, 2⅜) in / 4 (4, 4, 5, 6) cm above underarm, BO the center 37 (39, 39, 41, 41) sts for back neck and work each side separately. At neck edge, on every other row, BO 2,1 sts = 25 (26, 28, 29, 31) sts rem for each shoulder. When piece worked back and forth measures same length as half the measurement above underarm [= approx. 2⅜ (2⅜, 2½, 2½, 2¾) in / 6 (6, 6.5, 6.5, 7) cm], BO rem sts. The back now measures approx. 23¾ (24½, 25¼, 26, 26¾) in / 60 (62, 64, 66, 68) cm.

RIGHT FRONT
= 33 (34, 36, 37, 39) sts. Continue in pattern, working back and forth. *At the same time*, shape neck on every other row: BO 3,2,1,1,1, sts = 25 (26, 28, 29, 31) sts rem for shoulder. BO rem sts when front is same length as back.

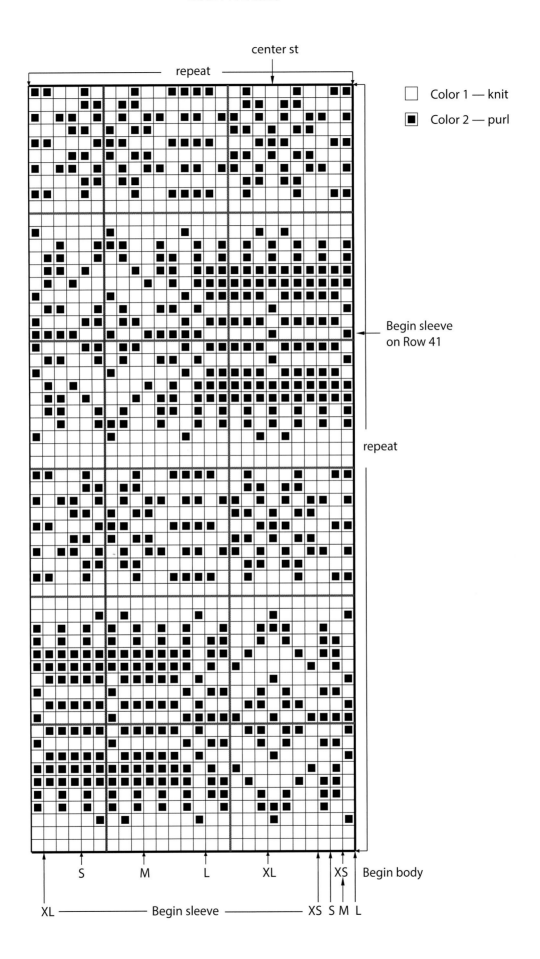

center st

repeat

Color 1 — knit

■ Color 2 — purl

Begin sleeve
on Row 41

repeat

S   M   L   XL   XS   Begin body

XL ——————— Begin sleeve ——————— XS S M L

LEFT FRONT
= 33 (34, 36, 37, 39) sts. Work as for right front, reversing shaping to match.

FINISHING
Join shoulders and sew sleeve caps to top of armholes inside 1 edge st. Make sure that center st on each sleeve matches shoulder seam. Seam underarms. Lightly steam press seams on WS under a damp pressing cloth. Also gently steam press lower edges of body and sleeves.

NECKBAND
With Color 1 and smaller circular, beginning at left shoulder pick up and knit 108 (108, 108, 112, 112) sts around neck. Knit 1 rnd and pm at each shoulder. Continue in **seed st in the round**: *Work Rnd 1 with Color 1, and Rnd 2 with Color 2*; rep * to * 3 more times. *At the same time,* decrease 1 st on each side of each marker on every other rnd a total of 4 times = 92 (92, 92, 96, 96) sts rem. Finish neckband with Color 1: knit 2 rnds, purl 1 rnd for foldline. Continue in stockinette for facing, increasing 1 st with M1 on each side of each marker on every other rnd a total of 4 times = 108 (108, 108, 112, 112) sts. Work facing until it is same length as neckband. BO loosely. Turn along foldline and loosely sew down edge on WS.

Weave in all ends neatly on WS. Lightly steam press neckband on WS under a damp pressing cloth.

FLORA PULLOVER

For this pullover, with its straight, wide silhouette, I chose a big organic pattern with long floats to try out a technique with a purled pattern against a stockinette background. The color choice is subdued. When the strands are twisted around each other on the long floats, some extra color spots appear in the purl pattern. The stockinette surface appears a bit uneven on a closer inspection. Overall, the look is visually interesting.

neckband on WS under a damp pressing cloth.

SKILL LEVEL
Experienced

SIZES
XS (S, M, L, XL)

FINISHED MEASUREMENTS
Chest: approx. 39½ (43, 46, 49¾, 53) in / 100 (109, 117, 126, 135) cm
Total Length: approx. 24½ (25¼, 26, 26¾, 27½) in / 62 (64, 66, 68, 70) cm
Sleeve Length: approx. 19¾ (20, 20, 20½, 20½) in / 50 (51, 51, 52, 52) cm

YARNS
CYCA #3 (DK, light worsted) Du Store Alpakka Sterk (40% finest alpaca, 40% Merino wool, 20% nylon, 150 yd/137 m / 50 g)
CYCA #3 (DK, light worsted) Dale Garn Pure Eco Wool (70% organic wool, 30% alpaca, 122 yd/112 m / 50 g)

YARN COLORS AND AMOUNTS
Color 1: Sterk Light Beige 845: 350 (400, 450, 450, 500) g
Color 2: Eco Wool Light Gray Heather 1202: 350 (400, 450, 450, 500) g

SUGGESTED NEEDLE SIZES
U. S. sizes 4 and 6 / 3.5 and 4 mm: long and short circulars and sets of 5 dpn

GAUGE
23 sts in patterned stockinette on larger needles = 4 in / 10 cm.
Adjust needle size to obtain correct gauge if necessary.

STITCHES AND TECHNIQUES

SEED STITCH IN THE ROUND
Rnd 1: *K1, p1*; rep * to * around.
Rnd 2: *P1, k1*; rep * to *around
Rep Rnds 1-2.

2-COLOR PATTERN IN KNIT AND PURL
Color 1 is worked in stockinette and Color 2 is purled throughout. Make sure that Color 2 lies on the back of the work as you knit. When there are long floats between colors, twist the colors around each other on WS every 5 or 6 stitches. Also, be careful not to stack the color twists to prevent the colors showing through on RS.

BODY
With Color 1 and smaller circular, CO 230 (250, 270, 290, 310) sts. Join, being careful not to twist cast-on row; pm for beginning of rnd. Work 3 rnds in **seed st** and then knit 1 rnd. Change to larger circular and pm at each side with 115 (125, 135, 145, 155) sts each for front and back. Work in pattern following chart. Begin at arrow for your size, knit to next side marker and then begin again at same arrow. Continue as est until body measures 21¼ (22, 22¾, 23¾, 24½) in /

SLEEVES

With Color 1 and smaller dpn, CO 58 (60, 62, 64, 66) sts. Divide sts onto 4 dpn and join, being careful not to twist cast-on row; pm for beginning of rnd. Work 2 rnds in **seed st** and then knit 1 rnd. Change to larger dpn and work in pattern following chart, beginning at arrow for your size. Pm at center of underarm. Every 1 (1, ¾, ¾, ¾) in / 2.5 (2.5, 2, 2, 2) cm, increase 1 st with M1 on each side of marker a total of 19 (20, 21, 22, 23) times = 96 100, 104, 108, 112) sts. Continue until sleeve measures 19¾ (20, 20, 20½, 20½) in / 50 (51, 51, 52, 52) cm. Knit 1 rnd with Color 1, turn sleeve inside out and knit 4 rnds for facing. BO loosely. Make second sleeve the same way.

FINISHING

Lightly steam press all pieces on WS under a damp pressing cloth. Measure width at top of a sleeve and then measure down from shoulder; mark bottom of armhole. Machine-stitch 2-3 fine straight lines on each side of center st on each side of body for armholes and on center front steek. Carefully cut each armhole and steek up center st. Seam shoulders. Attach sleeves; fold facings over cut edges and sew down loosely on WS. Lightly steam press sweater on WS under a damp pressing cloth.

NECKBAND

With Color 1 and smaller circular, beginning at left shoulder pick up and knit 92 (94, 96, 98, 100) sts around neck. Pm at each shoulder and knit 3 rnds. Work 3 rnds in **seed st** in the round. *At the same time*, decrease 1 st on each side of each marker on Rnds 3 and 6 = 84 (86, 88, 90, 92) sts rem. Knit 2 rnds, purl 1 rnd for foldline. Continue in stockinette for facing, increasing 1 st with M1 on each side of each marker on Rnds 3 and 6 = 92 (94, 96, 98, 100) sts. Work facing until it is same length as neckband. BO loosely. Turn along foldline and loosely sew down edge on WS.

Weave in all ends neatly on WS. Lightly steam press neckband on WS under a damp pressing cloth.

54 (56, 58, 60, 62) cm. BO the center front 15 (17, 19, 21, 23) sts for front neck. On next rnd, CO 3 sts over gap for center front steek. Steek sts are not included in pattern or stitch count. Continue around in pattern as est. *At the same time*, at neck edge, decrease on each side of steek as follows: 1 st on every rnd a total of 16 times. Before steek, decrease with k2tog tbl (or ssk); after steek, decrease with k2tog.

After completing decreases, 34 (38, 42, 46, 50) sts rem for each shoulder. Continue in pattern until body measures 24½ (25¼, 26, 26¾, 27½) in / 62 (64, 66, 68, 70) cm. Knit 1 rnd and then BO. The outermost 34 (38, 42, 46, 50) sts at each side of back are shoulder sts.

repeat

repeat

Color 1—knit

Color 2—purl

Begin
sleeve

XS S M L XL

Begin
body

XS　　S　　M　　L　　XL

⤴ LILY COWL AND WRIST WARMERS

For this set, I explored the technique of working the pattern with purl stitches on smaller needles and with two different types of yarn. The soft, slightly fuzzy alpaca yarn for the main color works well with a more traditional wool yarn. Combined, they will remind you of velvet. Both colors are deep, but the technique creates extra contrast in the pattern.

SKILL LEVEL
Experienced

SIZES
Women's

FINISHED MEASUREMENTS—COWL
Circumference: at lower edge, approx. 43 in / 109 cm; at upper edge, approx. 28¾ in / 73 cm
Length: approx. 15 in / 38 cm

FINISHED MEASUREMENTS—WRIST WARMERS
Circumference: approx. 7 in / 18 cm
Length: approx. 8 in / 20 cm

YARNS
CYCA #5 (Bulky) Du Store Alpakka Hexa (100% finest alpaca, 109 yd/100 m / 50 g)
CYCA #3 (DK, light worsted) Dale Garn Natural Lanolin Wool (100% pure new wool, 109 yd/100 m / 50 g)

YARN COLORS AND AMOUNTS
Cowl:
Color 1: Hexa Petroleum Heather 924: 150 g
Color 2: Lanolin Wool Dark Indigo Blue 1437: 100 g

Wrist Warmers:
Color 1: Hexa Petroleum Heather 924: 50 g
Color 2: Lanolin Wool Dark Indigo Blue 1437: 50 g

SUGGESTED NEEDLE SIZES
U. S. sizes 8 and 9 / 5 and 5.5 mm: long circulars and sets of 5 dpn

GAUGE
20 sts in pattern on larger needles = 4 in / 10 cm.
Adjust needle size to obtain correct gauge if necessary.

STITCHES AND TECHNIQUES

SEED STITCH IN THE ROUND
Rnd 1: *K1, p1*; rep * to * around.
Rnd 2: *P1, k1*; rep * to *around
Rep Rnds 1-2.

2-COLOR PATTERN IN KNIT AND PURL
Color 1 is worked in stockinette and Color 2 is purled throughout. Make sure that Color 2 lies on the back of the work as you knit. When there are long floats between colors, twist the colors around each other on WS every 5 or 6 stitches. Also, be careful not to stack these twists, to prevent the colors showing through on RS.

COWL

With Hexa and smaller circular, CO 218 sts. Join, being careful not to twist cast-on row; pm for beginning of rnd. Knit 1 rnd, work 2 rnds in **seed st**, and then knit 1 rnd. Pm at each side with 109 sts each for front and back. Change to larger circular and work in pattern following chart. **At the same time**, on Rnd 3, decrease 1 st at each side of each marker. Decrease with either p2tog or k2tog tbl depending on the pattern before each marker and p/k2tog after each marker = 4 sts decreased. Decrease the same way on every other rnd until you've decreased a total of 18 times = 146 sts rem.

147

COWL

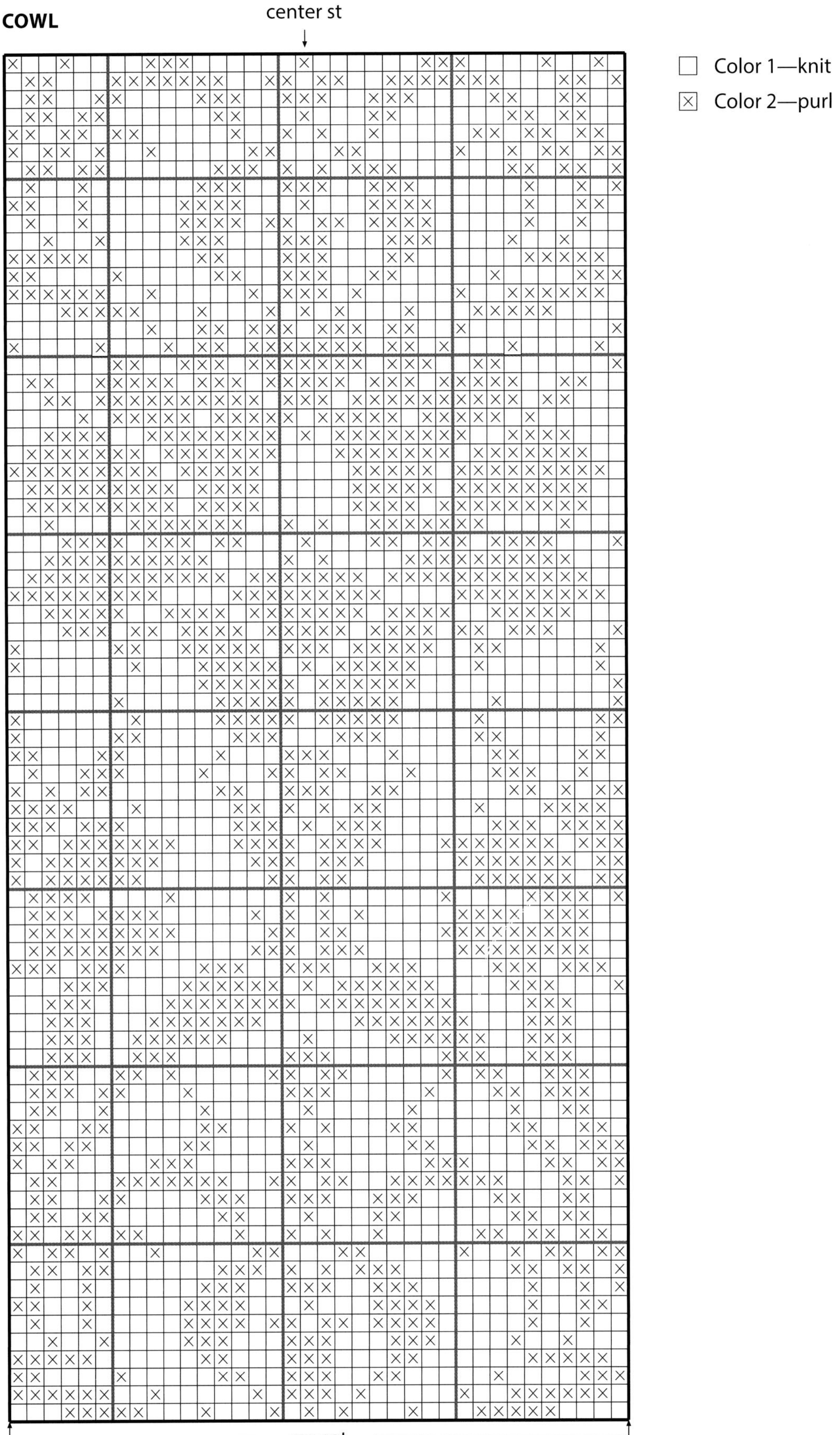
center st
repeat
Color 1—knit
Color 2—purl

WRIST WARMERS

With Hexa and smaller dpn, CO 37 sts. Divide sts onto dpn and join; pm for beginning of rnd. Knit 1 rnd, work 2 rnds in **seed st**, and then knit 1 rnd. Change to larger dpn and work in pattern following chart. After completing charted rows, with Hexa, knit 1 rnd, work 2 rnds **seed st**, knit 1 rnd. BO loosely—make sure edge is not too tight. Weave in all ends neatly on WS.

Continue without further decreases to end of chart and then change to smaller circular. With Hexa, knit 1 rnd, work 2 rnds **seed st**, knit 1 rnd. BO.

Weave in all ends neatly on WS. *Very gently* steam press the lower and upper edges on WS under a damp pressing cloth. You can wear the cowl with the sides with the decreases at the center front and back.

WRIST WARMERS

center st

☐ Color 1—knit
☒ Color 2—purl

♂ TUVA CABLED PULLOVER

This sweater is knitted with a combination of narrow twisted cables and a wide cable at center front and back and centered on each sleeve. A short, wide cut with a doubled high neckband gives the pullover a sturdy look.

SKILL LEVEL
Experienced

SIZES
XS (S, M, L, XL)

FINISHED MEASUREMENTS
Chest: approx. 36¼ (38½, 41¾, 45, 47¼) in / 92 (98, 106, 114, 120) cm
Total Length: approx. 21¼ (22, 22¾, 23¾, 24½) in / 54 (56, 58, 60, 62) cm
Sleeve Length: approx. 17¾ (18¼, 18½, 19, 19¼) in / 45 (46, 47, 48, 49) cm

YARNS
CYCA #3 (DK, light worsted) Dale Garn Natural Lanolin Wool (100% pure new wool, 109 yd/100 m / 50 g)
CYCA #0 (lace) Du Store Alpakka Dreamline Soul (68% baby alpaca, 32% nylon, 195 yd/177 m / 25 g)

YARN COLORS AND AMOUNTS
Lanolin Wool Dark Indigo Blue 1437: 700 (750, 800, 900, 1,000) g
Soul Purple Heather 210: 200 (225, 250, 275, 300) g

SUGGESTED NEEDLE SIZES
U. S. size 9 / 5.5 mm: long and short circulars and set of 5 dpn; cable needle
U. S. size 7 / 4.5 mm: long circular and set of 5 dpn

GAUGE
26 sts in Cable **A** on larger needles = 4 in / 10 cm.
22 sts in Cables **B** and **C** on larger needles = 4 in / 10 cm.
Adjust needle size to obtain correct gauge if necessary.

Note: Throughout, the sweater is worked with 1 strand each Lanolin Wool and Soul held together. Make sure you catch both yarns as you knit!

BODY
With both yarns held together and smaller circular, CO 212 (228, 244, 260, 276) sts. Join, being careful not to twist cast-on row. Pm at each side with 106 (114, 122, 130, 138) sts each for front and back. Set up cables as follows: *P1, work 36 (40, 44, 48, 52) sts following Chart **B**, work Chart **A** (= 32 sts), work 36 (40 44, 48, 52) sts following Chart **C**, p1* (= front); rep * to * (= back).

Work 6 rnds as est and then change to larger circular. Continue as est until body measures 9¾ (10¼, 10¾, 11, 11½) in / 25 (26, 27, 28, 29) cm. BO 8 sts at each side (= 4 sts on each side of each marker) = 98 (106, 114, 122, 130) sts rem each for front and back. Set body aside while you knit the sleeves.

SLEEVES
With both yarns held together and smaller dpn, CO 52 (52, 56, 56, 60) sts. Divide sts onto 4 dpn and join, being careful not to twist cast-on row; pm for beginning of rnd.
Set up cables as follows: Work 10 (10 12, 12, 14) sts following Chart **B**, work Chart **A** (= 32) sts, work 10 (10 12, 12, 14) sts following Chart **C**. Work 6 rnds as est and then change to larger dpn. Pm at center of underarm and increase 1 st with M1 on each side of marker every ¾ in / 2 cm a total of 20 (22, 22, 24, 24) times = 92 (96, 100, 104, 108) sts. Continue in pattern until sleeve measures 17¾ (18¼, 18½, 19, 19¼) in / 45 (46, 47, 48, 49) cm.

Note: Make sure that sleeve ends on same row of Chart **A** as body.

BO 8 sts at each side (= 4 sts on each side of marker) = 84 (88, 92, 96, 100) sts rem. Make second sleeve the same way.

YOKE

Place all the pieces on larger circular as follows: left sleeve, front, right sleeve, and back = 364 (388, 412, 436, 460) sts total. The rnd now begins between back and left sleeve. Continue in pattern and pm around 1 st at each intersection of sleeve and body (= pm around st on front and back) = 4 markers.

Note: Always purl the marked st.

At the same time, on Rnd 2, begin raglan decreases at all 4 marked sts as follows: Work until 2 sts before marked st, sl 1, k/p1 depending on pattern, psso, purl marked st, k/p2tog depending on pattern = 8 sts decreased around. Decrease the same way on *every other* rnd until you've decreased a total of 21 (23, 25, 27, 28) times = 196 (204, 212, 220, 228) sts rem. Now decrease on *every* rnd a total of 1 (2, 3, 4, 4) times = 188 (188, 188, 188, 196) sts rem.

Work 1 rnd without decreasing and cut yarn. Place 34 sts at center front on a holder for neck. The rnd now begins after the 34 sts. Work back and forth. Make sure to cross cables on RS rows. Continue raglan decreasing on *every* row until 34 sts rem on each sleeve. Stop decreasing on sleeves but continue decreases on front and back on *every* row until 34 (36, 38, 40, 44) sts rem on back and 0 (1, 2, 3, 5) st rem on each front. Work until cables come up to *same row* as those on stitch holder.

NECKBAND

Work the neckband in the round on larger circular. Place held front neck sts on needle and pick up and purl 5 sts on each side of these sts = 146 (150, 154, 158, 166) sts. Work and decrease in the purl sections between the cables as follows: P2tog on every rnd until 1 purl st rem at each side = 136 sts rem (all sizes). Work until neckband measures approx. 2 in / 5 cm. Turn work and work knit over purl and purl over knit. Work cables following Chart **A** for approx. 10¾ in / 27 cm. Work to and including Row 4 or 8 on chart and then BO.

FINISHING

Seam underarms.
Weave in all ends neatly on WS.

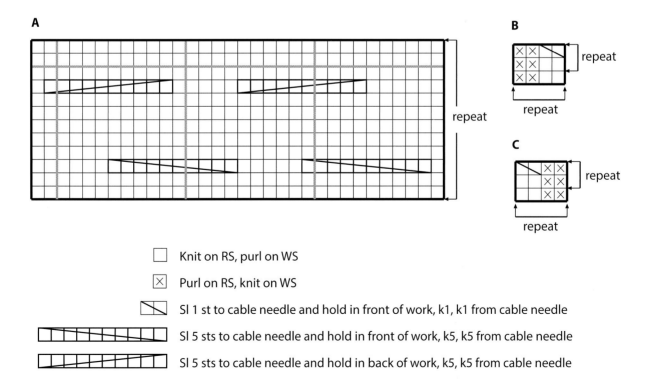

Knit on RS, purl on WS

Purl on RS, knit on WS

Sl 1 st to cable needle and hold in front of work, k1, k1 from cable needle

Sl 5 sts to cable needle and hold in front of work, k5, k5 from cable needle

Sl 5 sts to cable needle and hold in back of work, k5, k5 from cable needle

⚕ MAYA CABLED PULLOVER

The combination of several types of cables and reverse stockinette give this sweater a light look. This loose-fit pullover is finished with a high, simple cable neckband.

SKILL LEVEL
Experienced

SIZES
XS (S, M, L, XL)

FINISHED MEASUREMENTS
Chest: approx. 39½ (42¼, 45, 47¾, 50½) in / 100 (107, 114, 121, 128) cm
Total Length: approx. 23¾ (24½, 25¼, 26, 26¾) in / 60 (62, 64, 66, 68) cm
Sleeve Length: approx. 19 (19¼, 19¾, 20, 20½) in / 48 (49, 50, 51, 52) cm

YARNS
CYCA #3 (DK, light worsted) Dale Garn Pure Eco Wool (70% organic wool, 30% alpaca, 122 yd/112 m / 50 g)
CYCA #0 (lace) Du Store Alpakka Dreamline Soul (68% baby alpaca, 32% nylon, 195 yd/177 m / 25 g)

YARN COLORS AND AMOUNTS
Eco Wool Burgundy 1222: 550 (650, 700, 750, 850) g
Soul Red Heather 215: 175 (200, 225, 250, 275) g

SUGGESTED NEEDLE SIZES
U. S. size 8 / 5 mm: long and short circulars and set of 5 dpn; cable needle
U. S. size 6 / 4 mm: long circular and set of 5 dpn

GAUGE
30 sts in Cable **A** on larger needles = 4 in / 10 cm.
24 sts in Cable **B** on larger needles = 4 in / 10 cm.
17 sts in stockinette on larger needles = 4 in / 10 cm.
Adjust needle size to obtain correct gauge if necessary.

Note: Throughout, the sweater is worked with 1 strand each Eco Wool and Soul held together. Make sure you catch both yarns as you knit!

BODY
With both yarns held together and smaller circular, CO 236 (248, 260, 272, 284) sts. Join, being careful not to twist cast-on row. Knit 1 rnd and pm at each side with 118 (124, 130, 136, 142) sts each for front and back. Set up cables as follows: *(K1tbl, p1) over 0 (3, 6, 9, 12) sts, work cables following Chart **A** (24 sts), Chart **B** (23 sts), Chart **A** (24 sts), Chart **B** (23 sts), Chart **A** (24 sts), (p1, k1tbl) over 0 (3, 6, 9, 12) sts* (= front); rep from * to * (= back). Work 11 rnds as est and then change to larger circular. Continue as est *but* purl across the sections that had been (k1tbl, p1).

When body measures 14½ (15, 15½, 15¾, 16¼) in / 37 (38, 39, 40, 41) cm, shape armholes: BO 8 sts at each side (= 4 sts on each side of each marker) = 110 (116, 122, 128, 134) sts rem each for front and back. Set body aside while you knit the sleeves.

SLEEVES
With both yarns held together and smaller dpn, CO 40 (48, 48, 56, 56) sts. Divide sts onto 4 dpn and join, being careful not to twist cast-on row; pm for beginning of rnd.
Knit 1 rnd and then set up cables as follows with Charts **A**, **C**, and **D**: Work 8 (12, 12, 16, 16) sts following Chart **C**, work Chart **A** (= 24 sts), 8 (12, 12, 16, 16) sts following Chart **D**. Work 11 rnds as est and then change to larger dpn. Continue in pattern following Chart **A** *but* work purl across the sections that had been worked from Charts **C** and **D**.

Pm at center of underarm and increase 1 st with M1 on each side of marker every 1 (1¼, 1, 1¼, 1¼) in / 2.5 (3, 2.5, 3, 3) cm a total of 16 (14, 16, 14, 16) times = 72 (76, 80, 84, 88) sts. Continue without further decreases until sleeve measures 19 (19¼, 19¾, 20, 20½) in / 48 (49, 50, 51, 52) cm.

Note: Make sure that sleeve ends on same row of Chart **A** as body.

BO 8 sts at each side (= 4 sts on each side of marker) = 64 (68, 72, 76, 80) sts rem. Make second sleeve the same way.

YOKE
Place all the pieces on larger circular as follows: left sleeve, front, right sleeve, and back = 348 (368, 388, 408, 428) sts total. The rnd now begins between back and left sleeve. Continue in pattern and pm around 1 st at each intersection of sleeve and body (= pm around st on front and back) (= 4 markers).

Note: Always knit the marked st.

At the same time, on Rnd 2, begin raglan decreases at all 4 marked sts as follows: Work until 2 sts before marked st, sl 1, k/p1 depending on pattern, psso, knit marked st, k/p2tog depending on pattern = 8 sts decreased around. Decrease the same way on every other rnd until you've decreased a total of 20 (22, 24, 26, 28) times = 188 (192, 196, 200, 204) sts rem. Each sleeve has 24 sts rem and will now be worked *without* further decreases. Continue raglan decreases on front and back on *every* rnd a total of 10 times = 148 (152, 156, 160, 164) sts rem.

Work 1 rnd without decreasing and cut yarn. Place 28 sts at center front on a holder for neck. The rnd now begins after the 28 sts. Work back and forth. Make sure to cross cables on RS rows. On front and back, continue raglan decreasing on *every* row until 30 sts rem on back and 1 st rem on each front (all sizes). Work until cables come up to *same row* as those on stitch holder.

NECKBAND
Work the neckband in the round on larger circular.

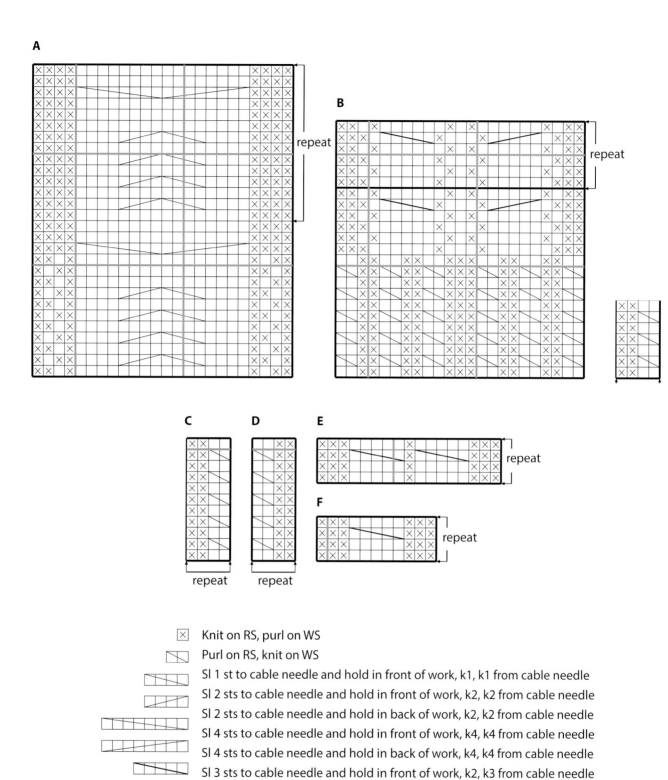

A

B

C **D** **E**

F

⊠	Knit on RS, purl on WS
⬚	Purl on RS, knit on WS
	Sl 1 st to cable needle and hold in front of work, k1, k1 from cable needle
	Sl 2 sts to cable needle and hold in front of work, k2, k2 from cable needle
	Sl 2 sts to cable needle and hold in back of work, k2, k2 from cable needle
	Sl 4 sts to cable needle and hold in front of work, k4, k4 from cable needle
	Sl 4 sts to cable needle and hold in back of work, k4, k4 from cable needle
	Sl 3 sts to cable needle and hold in front of work, k2, k3 from cable needle
	Sl 2 sts to cable needle and hold in back of work, k3, k2 from cable needle

Place held front neck sts on needle and pick up and purl 6 sts on each side of these sts = 120 sts. Work cable following Chart **A** as before. Work cable following Chart **E** on each side of Cable **A** on front and Chart **F** on each side of Cable **A** on back. Work as

est until neckband measures approx. 4-4¾ in / 10-12 cm. BO.

FINISHING

Seam underarms. Weave in all ends neatly on WS.

TIPS AND SHORTCUTS

GAUGE

Gauge is the most important aspect of your project before you begin to knit.

In order for the garment you want to knit to have the correct measurements and shaping, it's important that your gauge match that given in the pattern. If you knit more loosely than the given gauge, your garment will be larger than the measurements in the pattern; if you knit more tightly, the garment will be smaller. Everyone knits differently and that affects the finished garment.

Take the time to check your gauge before you begin the project. It can save you a lot of time and frustration. Make a gauge swatch with 6-8 more stitches than the given gauge. Work a minimum of 1½-2 in / 4-5 cm. Count the number of stitches in 4 in / 10 cm. If you have more stitches than given, try larger needles. If you have fewer stitches, change to smaller needles.

Several of the sweaters in this book have both single-color stockinette and two-color stranded patterns. If you work stranded knitting more tightly than stockinette, go up a needle size or two for the best results possible.

The needle sizes given in the patterns are only recommendations. Try different sizes to see what works best or to decide if you need to go up or down on needle size.

MEASUREMENTS

To find your size:
1. Measure a garment that fits you well.
2. Compare those measurements with those in the pattern.
3. Choose the size based on the chest measurements in the pattern.
4. The length of the body and sleeves can be lengthened or shortened as necessary.

Always measure the garment lying flat—lay it on a table or the floor. Never measure the garment on a sofa or chair. Smooth out but do not stretch the garment.

FLOATS IN TWO-COLOR STRANDED KNITTING

With long floats (strands behind the work between two colors) should be twisted about every 4 stitches, depending on the pattern. Make sure not to stack the twists or the yarn will show on the right side.

INCREASING AND DECREASING

INCREASING without holes: Pick up the strand between 2 stitches, lift strand onto left needle and knit into back loop to twist strand = M1 (make 1).

Decreasing at Markers

The neatest decreases are mirror-image pairs that lean towards each other: knit 2 together through back loops or ssk BEFORE the marker and knit 2 together AFTER the marker.

Decreasing in Lace Patterns

Pay attention to the lace pattern when decreasing. If the decrease comes in the middle of a paired yarnover and decrease, instead, work those stitches in stockinette, a relief pattern, or in the given pattern.

Increasing in Lace Patterns

Pay attention to the lace pattern when increasing. If the increase comes in the middle of a paired yarnover and decrease, work those stitches in stockinette, a relief pattern, or in the given pattern instead.

Binding Off

Do not bind off too tightly—the bound-off edge should have the same tension and width as the rest of the piece.

All of the bind-off methods described below are

repeated until 1 st remains. Cut yarn and draw end through last stitch loop.

1. Slip 1 stitch, knit 1 stitch, pass slipped stitch over.

2. Knit 2 stitches together, slip stitch back to left needle.

3. Double decrease: Slip 1 stitch, knit 2 stitches together, pass first stitch over the two together. This bind-off method is especially good for ribbing.

WEAVING IN OR FASTENING OFF ENDS

Sometimes it's best to weave in ends diagonally; other times, vertically. It depends on the yarn/structure. Don't trim the ends too short or they might loosen from the fabric with wear. It's also important to make sure woven ends don't show on the right side. Heavy yarn can be split and each ply woven in separately.

KNOTS IN YARN AND SPLICING

Sometimes knots show up in yarn. In that case, you should undo the knot and splice the yarn. Make sure the splice is as invisible as possible. As a general rule, it is best to make a join at a side edge. *Do not make a join in the middle of a row.*

FINISHING

For your results to come out looking tidy, finishing is at least as important as the knitting itself.

STEAM BLOCKING

Some yarns will tolerate steam well, and it will make the fibers lofty. Other yarns have to be steamed very carefully or not at all. If nothing is stated about steam pressing in the instructions, it means that the piece should not be steam blocked. Sometimes, you will steam press the entire garment, sometimes only the seams. Always use a damp pressing cloth when you steam press, and press only on the wrong side of the knitting. Dip the garment in clean water and gently squeeze out excess water so that the fabric feels damp but not wet. Use a warm iron but be careful not to press too hard because that will make the piece flat and lifeless. How much a garment can be steamed also depends on the knitted structure. Always lay a garment flat to dry and leave it until completely dry before seaming.

SEAMING GARMENTS

Sew pieces together with seams as narrow as possible. Sew into each stitch for smooth results and make sure that the stitches and rows in the pattern/structure match at the sides and shoulders. Attach sleeves to the body with right side to right side. Work carefully as you seam so that the sleeve seams on front and back are straight and neat. Normally, you will seam with the same yarn as for knitting. A very heavy yarn can be split or you can use a finer yarn in a color matching as closely as possible. Always steam press the garment under a damp pressing cloth as a finishing touch.

KNITTING PIECES TOGETHER

Instead of sewing pieces together, you can knit them together. This technique is best for finishing straight garments. Place the stitches from one piece on a needle and the same number of stitches on another needle. Make sure the pieces face right side to right side.

Use a third needle to join the first stitch on each needle. You can bind off at the same time or bind off on the next row after all the pieces have been knitted together.

PICKING UP AND KNITTING STITCHES

It's easier to use a crochet hook instead of a knitting needle to pick up and knit stitches. Make sure that the stitches are correctly aligned on the needle when slipped from the crochet hook to the knitting needle.

ABBREVIATIONS

BO	bind off (= British cast off)		pm	place marker
CC	contrast (pattern) color		psso	pass slipped stitch over
ch	chain stitch		rem	remain(s)(ing)
cm	centimeters		rep	repeat
CO	cast on		RLI	right-lifted increase: knit into right side of st below st on needle and then knit st on needle
dpn	double-pointed needles			
in	inch(es)		RS	right side
g	grams		sc	single crochet (= British double crochet)
k	knit		sl	slip
k2tog	knit 2 together (= 1 stitch decreased; right-leaning decrease)		sl m	slip marker
			sl st	slip stitch
LLI	left-lifted increase: knit into left side of 2nd st below that on needle		ssk	[slip 1 knitwise] 2 times, knit the 2 sts together through back loops (= 1 stitch decreased; left-leaning decrease)
M1R	make 1 right = increase 1 stitch by picking up the strand between 2 stitches with left needle tip, from back to front and knit into front of strand		st(s)	stitch(es)
			tbl	through back loop(s)
			tog	together
			WS	wrong side
M1	make 1 or M1L = increase 1 stitch by picking up the strand between two stitches with the left needle tip, from front to back, and knit directly into back loop.This makes a left-leaning increase.		yb	with yarn held in back
			wyf	with yarn held in front
			yd	yard(s)
			yo	yarnover
			–	repeat the sequence between the asterisks
M1p	make 1 purlwise = increase 1 stitch by picking up the strand between two stitches with the left needle tip, from back to front, and purl directly into front loop (= right-leaning increase); for left-leaning increase, pick up strand from front to back and purl into back loop		Steek	A steek is a section of extra stitches added so that you can knit in the round on a sweater body that will later be cut open for the two fronts of a cardigan or for the arm holes from underarms to shoulders, or for the neck (for example, a placket). Usually the steek stitches are worked in alternating pattern colors or with one color for single-color rounds. Instructions for working the steek stitches and for reinforcing and cutting a steek are given in individual patterns.
m	meters			
MC	main (background) color			
mm	millimeters			
p	purl			

YARN RESOURCES

Thank you to all the yarn distributors who contributed yarn for this book

Brooklyn Tweed yarns may be purchased from retailers listed by:
BROOKLYN TWEED
www.brooklyntweed.com

Some Dale Garn yarns may be available from:
YARN CUPBOARD
yarncupboard.com

Some Hillesvåg yarns may be purchased (with international shipping charges) from:
YSOLDA
ysolda.com

Rauma yarns are available from:
THE YARN GUYS
theyarnguys.com

THE WOOLLY THISTLE
thewoollythistle.com

Some yarns and materials—Du Store Alpakka, Mondial, Trollkar, Værbitt, and Viking yarns, in particular—may be difficult to find. A variety of additional and substitute yarns are available from:
WEBS – AMERICA'S YARN STORE
75 Service Center Road
Northampton, MA 01060
800-367-9327
yarn.com

LOVEKNITTING.COM
loveknitting.com/us

If you are unable to obtain any of the yarn used in this book, it can be replaced with a yarn of a similar weight and composition. Please note, however, the finished projects may vary slightly from those shown, depending on the yarn used. Try www.yarnsub.com for suggestions.

For more information on selecting or substituting yarn, contact your local yarn shop or an online store; they are familiar with all types of yarns and would be happy to help you. Additionally, the online knitting community at Ravelry.com has forums where you can post questions about specific yarns. Yarns come and go so quickly these days and there are so many beautiful yarns available.